The Legislature of Brazil

T0386218

This book develops a critical analysis of the Brazilian legislature, specifically the role of its lower chamber, the Chamber of Deputies, in policy-making and how this combines with its public engagement role, namely in terms of promoting participation and transparency. The book draws from Nelson Polsby's theoretical conceptualisation about transformative and arena legislatures. The purpose is not to reach a consensus about the exact categorisation of the legislature in Polsby's classification. On the contrary, the chapters are mainly concerned in challenging this classification through interdisciplinary perspectives drawn from within the legislative studies in Brazil.

The book's first chapters introduce the reader to a historical overview of the Brazilian legislature's policy-making and organisation, identifying its role in proposing public policies and scrutinising proposals from the Executive Branch. The subsequent chapters focus on its public engagement role and address contemporary elements – such as political participation and transparency – and how these interlink, or not, with legislative practices and influence the production of law. The book provides a unique insight into the operation and power of the legislature of a key global power, Brazil, in a presidential political system context.

The chapters were originally published as a special issue in *The Journal of Legislative Studies*.

Cristiane Brum Bernardes gained her PhD in Political Science (2010) at the Institute of Social and Political Studies (IESP), University of State of Rio de Janeiro (UERJ), Brazil. She also has a Master's in Communication and Information from the Federal University of Rio Grande do Sul, Brazil (2004). She is a Senior Lecturer of the Legislative Affairs Master's Programme of the Brazilian Chamber of Deputies.

Cristina Leston-Bandeira is Professor of Politics, University of Leeds, UK. She is also co-convenor of the Parliaments and Legislatures Specialist Group of the Political Studies Association and editor of *Parliaments and Citizens* (Routledge, 2013).

Ricardo de João Braga gained his PhD in Political Science (2011) from the University of State of Rio de Janeiro (UERJ), Brazil. He is a Senior Lecturer of the Legislative Affairs Master's Programme of the Brazilian Chamber of Deputies. Previously, he worked for party leaderships in the Brazilian Chamber of Deputies and for the Executive Branch.

Library of Legislative Studies

Edited by
Lord Philip Norton of Louth, *University of Hull, UK*

For a complete list of titles please visit https://www.routledge.com/Library-of-Legislative-Studies/book-series/LLS

The Internet and Parliamentary Democracy in Europe
A Comparative Study of the Ethics of Political Communication in the Digital Age
Edited by Xiudian Dai and Philip Norton

Parliamentary Opposition in Old and New Democracies
Edited by Ludger Helms

Post-Communist Parliaments
The second decade
Edited by David M. Olson and Gabriella Ilonszki

Ceremony and Ritual in Parliament
Edited by Shirin M. Rai

The Roles and Function of Parliamentary Questions
Edited by Shane Martin and Olivier Rozenberg

Post-Communist Parliaments
Change and stability in the second decade
Edited by David M. Olson and Gabriella Ilonszki

Parliaments and Citizens
Edited by Cristina Leston-Bandeira

Legislatures of Small States
A Comparative Study
Edited by Nicholas D. J. Baldwin

Parliamentary Communication in EU Affairs
Connecting with the Electorate?
Edited by Katrin Auel and Tapio Raunio

Government-Opposition in Southern European Countries during the Economic Crisis
Great Recession, Great Cooperation?
Edited by Elisabetta De Giorgi and Catherine Moury

The Legislature of Brazil
An Analysis of Its Policy-making and Public Engagement Roles
Edited by Cristiane Brum Bernardes, Cristina Leston-Bandeira and Ricardo de João Braga

The Legislature of Brazil

An Analysis of Its Policy-Making and
Public Engagement Roles

Edited by
**Cristiane Brum Bernardes,
Cristina Leston-Bandeira and
Ricardo de João Braga**

Routledge
Taylor & Francis Group

LONDON AND NEW YORK

First published 2018 by Routledge

2 Park Square, Milton Park, Abingdon, Oxfordshire OX14 4RN
52 Vanderbilt Avenue, New York, NY 10017

Routledge is an imprint of the Taylor & Francis Group, an informa business

First issued in paperback 2019

British Library Cataloguing in Publication Data
A catalogue record for this book is available from the British Library

ISBN 13: 978-1-138-55528-0 (hbk)
ISBN 13: 978-0-367-89201-2 (pbk)

Typeset in Minion Pro
by diacriTech, Chennai

Publisher's Note
The publisher accepts responsibility for any inconsistencies that may have arisen during
the conversion of this book from journal articles to book chapters, namely the possible
inclusion of journal terminology.

Disclaimer
Every effort has been made to contact copyright holders for their permission to reprint
material in this book. The publishers would be grateful to hear from any copyright
holder who is not here acknowledged and will undertake to rectify any errors or
omissions in future editions of this book.

Contents

CONTENTS

Citation Information

The chapters in this book were originally published in *The Journal of Legislative Studies*, volume 22, issue 4 (December 2016). When citing this material, please use the original page numbering for each article, as follows:

Introduction
Cristiane Brum Bernardes, Cristina Leston-Bandeira and Ricardo de João Braga
The Journal of Legislative Studies, volume 22, issue 4 (December 2016) pp. 445–459

Chapter 1
The institutionalisation of the Brazilian Chamber of Deputies
Ricardo de João Braga, André Rehbein Sathler and Roberto Campos da Rocha Miranda
The Journal of Legislative Studies, volume 22, issue 4 (December 2016) pp. 460–483

Chapter 2
The legislative and public policies in Brazil: before and after the 1988 Constitution
Julio Roberto de Souza Pinto
The Journal of Legislative Studies, volume 22, issue 4 (December 2016) pp. 484–505

Chapter 3
The role of the Brazilian Congress in defining public social policies
Fábio de Barros Correia Gomes and Ricardo Chaves de Rezende Martins
The Journal of Legislative Studies, volume 22, issue 4 (December 2016) pp. 506–527

CITATION INFORMATION

Chapter 4

Green or grey: origin, bias and fate of environmental bills in the Brazilian National Congress
Maurício Schneider and Ana Alice Biedzicki de Marques
The Journal of Legislative Studies, volume 22, issue 4 (December 2016)
pp. 528–539

Chapter 5

Brazilian Parliament and digital engagement
Antonio Teixeira de Barros, Cristiane Brum Bernardes and Malena Rehbein
The Journal of Legislative Studies, volume 22, issue 4 (December 2016)
pp. 540–558

Chapter 6

Open parliament policy applied to the Brazilian Chamber of Deputies
Cristiano Faria and Malena Rehbein
The Journal of Legislative Studies, volume 22, issue 4 (December 2016)
pp. 559–578

Conclusion

Cristiane Brum Bernardes, Cristina Leston-Bandeira and Ricardo de João Braga
The Journal of Legislative Studies, volume 22, issue 4 (December 2016)
pp. 579–583

For any permission-related enquiries please visit:
http://www.tandfonline.com/page/help/permissions

Notes on Contributors

Antonio Teixeira de Barros has a PhD in Sociology and is a Senior Lecturer of the Legislative Affairs Master's Programme of the Brazilian Chamber of Deputies.

Cristiane Brum Bernardes has a PhD in Political Science and is a Senior Lecturer of the Legislative Affairs Master's Programme of the Brazilian Chamber of Deputies.

Ana Alice Biedzicki de Marques is currently Director of Sustainable Use of Biodiversity and Forests at IBAMA (the Brazilian Federal Environmental agency).

Ricardo de João Braga gained his PhD in Political Science (2011) from the University of State of Rio de Janeiro (UERJ), Brazil. He is a Senior Lecturer of the Legislative Affairs Master's Programme of the Brazilian Chamber of Deputies.

Fábio de Barros Correia Gomes is a legislative consultant (on health policy matters) at the Brazilian Chamber of Deputies (BCD) (since 2003) and has taught at the BCD's Master on Legislative Power since 2013.

Cristiano Faria has a PhD in Political Science and is a Senior Lecturer of the Legislative Affairs Master's Programme of the Brazilian Chamber of Deputies.

Cristina Leston-Bandeira is Professor of Politics, University of Leeds, UK. She is also co-convenor of the Parliaments and Legislatures Specialist Group of the Political Studies Association and editor of *Parliaments and Citizens* (Routledge, 2013).

Ricardo Chaves de Rezende Martins is a legislative consultant (on education policy matters) at the Brazilian Chamber of Deputies (since 1991) and has taught at the BCD's Master on Legislative Branch since 2013.

Roberto Campos da Rocha Miranda has an Information Science PhD and is a legislative analyst in human resources affairs.

NOTES ON CONTRIBUTORS

Julio Roberto de Souza Pinto is a lawyer, has a PhD in Sociology from the University of Brasilia, Brazil, and is a Senior Lecturer of the Legislative Affairs Master's Programme of the Brazilian Chamber of Deputies.

Malena Rehbein is a civil servant at the Brazilian Chamber of Deputies, where she works as a journalist and is a Senior Lecturer of the Legislative Affairs Master's Programme of the Brazilian Chamber of Deputies.

André Rehbein Sathler is Vice President at the University Centre Izabela Hendrix, Brazil, and analyst at the Brazilian Chamber of Deputies.

Maurício Schneider is a biologist working as a senior specialist in Environmental Law and Environmental Policy at the Office of Legislative Counsel and Policy Guidance of the Chamber of Deputies, Brazil, and a former research fellow at the University of East Anglia, UK.

Introduction

Cristiane Brum Bernardes, Cristina Leston-Bandeira and Ricardo de João Braga

ABSTRACT
This special issue of The *Journal of Legislative Studies* focuses on the Brazilian Parliament's lower chamber, the Chamber of Deputies. Its core concern is with its representative role, in the way it articulates policy-making capacity and interaction between citizens and parliament. In this Introduction we outline an historical and systemic profile of the Brazilian parliament before presenting our analytical framework. Our theoretical framework makes use of Polsby's typology on Arena and Transformative legislatures, to situate our study of the wider representative role of the Chamber of Deputies. We finish by presenting the volume's substantive chapters.

Brazilian's lower chamber

This special issue of *The Journal of Legislative Studies* focuses on the Brazilian Parliament's lower chamber, the Chamber of Deputies. Our core concern is with representation, as a central component of the Legislative Branch in Brazil, both in its practical actions and its normative framework. We address the representative function through a dual approach: public policy and the relationship between the public and the institution. As such, the first set of articles relate to the production of public policies in the Brazilian presidentialism context, and the second regards the interaction between citizens and parliament and the new communication and information technologies applied to the Legislative Branch.

Despite its image to the world as a young nation and as a democracy undergoing its consolidation process, Brazil's political history is significant and explanatory of its present. The fragility of representation on different occasions, the institutional ruptures, and the consequent instability of democracy for long periods mould the operation of the Chamber of Deputies.

This introduction aims to provide an overall framework briefly explaining Brazilian's political system, as well as outlining our theoretical framework, which is then followed by subsequent articles. It also briefly introduces the issue's articles.

Brazil: political history and democracy

Brazil is a fairly extensive country (8.5 million km^2, approximately, a little smaller than Europe), boasting a population a little over 200 million people (Brasil, 2016). Located in the eastern part of South America, its history is linked to the maritime European explorations of the Renaissance, with its colonisation by Portugal. Its population is comprised of black people (brought as slaves from Africa), white Europeans of several nationalities and indigenous people (Freyre, 2001). The economy of the country, for most of its history, has been based on primary products offered to the external market, and, from the 1930s onward, it developed a manufacturing industry and broadened its fields of action (Furtado, 2008; Prado, 1970).

In political terms, Brazilian history gains more significance with independence from Portugal, which occurred in 1822. The Chamber of Deputies was created in 1824 by the first Constitution of Brazil (bestowed by the Emperor, D. Pedro I) and formed a Bicameral National Legislative System, along with the Senate, which continued in activity throughout the Empire and remained during the Republic (established in 1889).

During the Empire, the country was ruled as a constitutional monarchy, which gained parliamentary aspects in the 1840s, when the second regent assumed power, D. Pedro II. During the Empire, Senate was for life and provided the key staffers of the ministry offices. The Chamber of Deputies, on its part, was elected, but the elections were not free, clean, or representative. Usually the Emperor would choose the Office and the elections were performed later, as a pure formal instrument during which many frauds occurred.

With the Republic, presidentialism was established, the Senate came to be elected and the political organisation of the country became a federal affair. Presidentialism is the regime in which the Executive Branch is elected independently from the Legislative Branch. The Executive does not need the formal support of the Legislative Branch to survive; on the other hand, the Legislative Branch cannot be dissolved by acts of the president, it has a fixed term.

The Federal State is a characteristic of the Republic, but the strength of the political decentralisation oscillates during all the period. At the beginning of the Republic and during democratic periods the decentralisation is more pronounced; during authoritarian periods it is centralised in the president.

The Brazilian political history of the two most recent centuries has therefore suffered significant changes, many of them institutional ruptures. The institution of the Republic was one of them. The second one was the Vargas period, which, from 1930 to 1945 governed the country under two exception regimes (from 1930 to 1933 and from 1937 to 1945) and also under democratic rules (from 1934 to 1937). The third rupture was the military coup, which established an exception regime between 1964 and 1985. It is important to realise that both exception periods performed several institutional changes, such as political centralisation and extinction of preceding parties and political forces.

As elsewhere, the introduction of political participation to the popular masses represented a considerable social and economic change. Along with industrialisation and urbanisation, reinforced from 1930 onwards, the working class became subjects in their political and social rights through the hands of the dictator Vargas, who established labour regulations during his dictatorship and structured the political dispute between labourists and conservatives from 1945 onwards, with the institution of democracy. The fall of Vargas in 1945 was not its end, quite the opposite. His actions (he was president again between 1951 and 1954, and committed suicide during the course of his term) and his political image influenced the whole of the democratic period until 1964. In fact, it is only from 1930 onwards that a labourist ideology started to form (with political parties that represent left ideas, specifically after 1945) in opposition to a more conservative and older ideology. Owing to the institutional political fragility (the parties were not strong and the elections were peppered with frauds, for example) the mobilisation of the masses happened under what came to be known as *populismo* (Ianni, 1978; Weffort, 1980), which is the combination of low institutionalisation, personalisation of political leaderships and direct contact between leader and people. *Populismo* has been a feature of Brazil since then.

The National Congress – Brazil's Parliament – has been bicameral since the enactment of the first Constitution in 1824. The Federal Senate was the prevailing house since it boasted more prerogatives and more influential politicians during both the Empire and the Republic. During the Empire, the division of the legislative houses was inspired in the English template of one chamber for the people in general and another for noblemen. During the Republic, following an inspiration from the United States, the Federal Senate started representing the states of the Federation (Porto, 2002). During both centuries, we are talking about a strong bicameralism (Llanos & Nolte, 2003).

The electoral system applied to elections for the lower chamber have encompassed a few forms of majoritarian choice (uninominal and plurinominal districts) since the inception of the Empire until 1932, and from then on a proportional system was enacted (Pires, 2011). National parties with significance among the electors truly appeared after 1945. Until that time, Brazil had the experience of parties with no popular participation – with two main parties during the Empire (conservatives and liberals) and several republican state parties that did not compete among themselves from the end of the nineteenth century to 1930. Those parties were restricted to each state (the dominant ones came from São Paulo and Minas Gerais, the richest and more populated states).

Representative democracy as we know it currently came into existence in Brazil only after 1945, when a significant proportion of citizens started voting (alphabetised men and women had a right to vote) in free, competitive and relatively clean elections. From 1945 onwards, parties with a nationwide influence also appeared.

The 1964 military *coup d'état* was, according to a dominant interpretation (Santos, 1986), the peak of a process of polarisation and radicalisation of political forces between right and left. The right-wing position, supported by the military, developed under a mixture of nationalist and internationalist positions. During this period, political freedom was limited, and a somewhat particular template emerged: important politicians had their terms and political rights revoked, some popular movements, political rights and previous parties were suppressed, and direct elections for president and governors were extinguished. On the other hand, elections for the national Legislative Branch and for Executive and parliamentary roles in small towns were maintained, the Congress continued operating most of the time and the creation of two parties, Arena (National Renewal Alliance or Aliança Renovadora Nacional, in Portuguese) and MDB (Democratic Brazilian Movement or Movimento Democrático Brasileiro, in Portuguese), was allowed, with the latter being an opposition party.

The overview of this long historical process can be summarised by Figure 1, which presents the main events and characteristics of the Brazilian political system in the last two centuries.

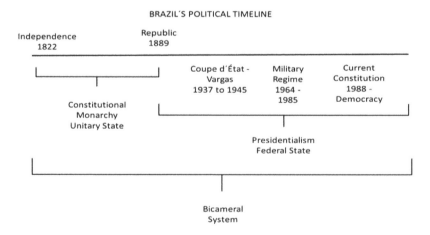

Figure 1. Political timeline of Brazil. Source: Developed by the authors.

4

The transition to democracy during the 1970s and 1980s of the twentieth century was slow (Marenco, 2007): new parties were allowed to be created from 1979 onwards, censorship was extinguished, political prisoners were granted amnesty and the elections became gradually direct again (governor in 1982 and president in 1989). A milestone of the democratisation was the enactment of the current Constitution, in 1988, stemming from a Constitution Assembly comprised of a majority that opposed the military regime. The new Constitution comprises several democratic principles and values and maintains the Federal State and presidentialism.[1]

The Chamber of Deputies and the Brazilian political system

Brazil has a presidential political system. Currently, the terms in Brazil comprise four years for all roles, except for the senators, who have an eight-year term.

The Chamber of Deputies currently boasts 513 elected representatives in its 27 federative units (26 states and a federal district), while the Senate has 81 parliamentarians, three for each unit. Senate elections happen through a majority system (elections of one and two senators, alternated every four years), and elections for the lower chamber happen by means of an open-list proportional system.

Independent electoral coalitions – not controlled by national caucuses – are allowed in each state and for each role, which causes two problems. The first one is a lack of unity and clarity of partisan positions in front of the voters and the second one, for the proportional process, is the election of candidates from minor parties that leverage their coalition with strong parties to achieve the electoral quotient (in Brazil, votes for the coalition are not split among the parties: the most voted for of the coalition are elected, regardless of their party). In the 2014 elections, for example, 28 parties were able to elect representatives for the Chamber of Deputies, which demonstrates a marked fragmentation.

Each state has a variable minimum number of seats in the Chamber of Deputies, according to its population. However, there is a minimum of eight and a maximum of 70 deputies established by the Constitution (medium size of 19) for each district/state (each state is an electoral district), which causes malapportionment issues that benefit the smaller, poorer and less populated states, which are over-represented.

The Brazilian political system encompasses an almost exclusive combination of key features: presidentialism, federalism, proportional electoral system (for the lower chamber) and multipartisanship. It has been a rule that the largest party is not able to obtain a majority in the Legislative Branch (from the 1990s onwards, none of the parties could form a majoritarian bench; the threshold hovered around 20 per cent of the chairs of the

Chamber and is falling – currently under 14 per cent). Thus, it is the president's job to build a multipartisan legislative coalition to support their government programme. Therefore, the creation of majorities always demands a significant number of parties. As a major consequence of this there is a huge party fragmentation which hampers the construction of the government, affecting specifically the legislative coalition that supports the Executive agenda and weakens citizens' capacity to identify parties and their position relative to government.

The hegemonic interpretation in Brazil today is that our presidentialist system is similar to the parliamentarian system in the sense that a government coalition is formed, headed by the president of the Republic, and this coalition supports the legislative presidential agenda and exerts ministry (the Presidential Office). In this system, we treat it as a coalition presidentialism (Abranches, 1988; Braga & Guimarães, 2015; Power, 2015), which historically has presented significant levels of discipline inside the Legislature and success of the Executive Branch in leading the government agenda (Figueiredo & Limongi, 2001).

The current Brazilian Constitution created rules in which the prerogatives of the president of the Republic were maintained, with minor changes, regarding budgeting and public administration (prerogatives that were expanded during the previous military regime). In the current democratic ruling, only the president is capable of proposing the budget and of creating or extinguishing public administration offices. The legislators have a small margin to change the budget, through the expansion of revenue predictions, but they are able to influence only minimally the actions of the Executive Branch. As a consequence, deputies depend on the presidential power to develop their political careers, and the president can control them, managing a sort of favours and opportunities.

The agenda of the Legislative Branch is strongly controlled by the Executive Branch, which has effective power in defining political debate at each moment. The president of the Republic is able to put forth temporary measures (Medidas Provisórias), which are immediately effective decrees that the Legislature has to assess within a fixed deadline. The assessment of temporary measures by the Legislature is imposed, subject to the penalty of impairment of the assessment of other matters while they are not assessed. Law projects urgently requested by the president of the Republic also block the legislative agenda; however, they are not immediately effective and have to be approved by the Legislative Branch. The president of the Republic is also able to present Proposals for Amendment of the Constitution, which are important, since the Brazilian Carta Magna is very ample and regulates many activities. Since 1988, the president of the Republic has broadly enjoyed these prerogatives.

Among the variety of organisational and institutional formats of legislatures all over the world, Brazil is probably among the ones with considerable financial and human resources (Guimarães, Schwartz, Souza, & Melo, 2015) and among those with medium legislative prerogatives and activities. There is, therefore, some discrepancy between the large size and complex structure of the Chamber of Deputies and its limited effective power over national politics and the making of public policies.

The Brazilian Parliament is a huge organisation that integrates the classical political roles of a parliament, that is, legislate, enforce and represent,[2] with a number of support or concurrent activities besides the political ones. The Brazilian Parliament is among those with larger infrastructures (like the United States' one), standing out in its high ratio between employees/parliamentarians.[3] Along with the assessment of matters and parliamentary debates are a few differentiating characteristics when compared with the international scene, such as the extensive structures for interaction and communication with society (both with traditional and digital media) and the large physical, logistic and support staff available for parliamentarians (with staff and space allocated for the political offices of the house, for the partisan leaderships, and also for the individual offices[4]).

The Chamber of Deputies has a floor space of approximately 150,000 square metres. On the days with the most flow, 20,000–30,000 citizens pass through it (Medeiros et al., 2011) and it has approximately 15,000 employees.[5] It has an approximate annual budget of R$ 5 billion (2016). Both the lower chamber and the Federal Senate have, each, a structure with a library, security services, legislative TV, legislative radio, news agency, technical advisors, and an extensive managerial structure geared towards the administration of spaces, property, finances and personnel.

The theoretical framework

Twenty-five years ago the discussion of Brazilian political science revolved around the governability of the political system – the concept of 'coalition presidentialism' created by Abranches (1988) to define the Brazilian political system in action is the best example of this concern. An answer for the persistent and important question posed by Linz (1994): to know whether presidentialist systems such as the Brazilian one were governable.

A series of works based on the neo-institutionalism of the Rational Choice, supported by empirical research and dialogue with the literature of legislative studies, both national and non-Brazilian and spearheaded by the works of Argelina Figueiredo and Fernando Limongi (Figueiredo & Limongi, 1995, 1997, 2001, 2008; Figueiredo, Limongi, & Valente, 1999; Limongi & Figueiredo, 1998), demonstrated that Brazil, indeed, was governable. The Legislative Branch has not prevented the approval of a government programme conducted by the Executive Branch, but has cooperated with it. The explanation is that the president of the Republic counts on important legislative resources to conduct the government programme within the Legislature, and the distribution of roles in the Office and of budgetary resources among the parties solidifies the coalition. Still, the centralised decision-making structure of the Legislative Branch, centred in the president of the Chamber of Deputies, the president of the Federal Senate and the partisan leaderships, helps the negotiations of the Executive Branch, since it is restricted to just a few actors.

This explanation has been submitted to academic criticisms in theoretical and empirical terms that question the enforcement capacity of the political institutions to guarantee stability and success to presidents (Palermo, 2000; Renno, 2006). But the three presidents elected from 1994 onwards, who not only performed their terms but also were re-elected (four-year terms with the possibility of a re-election), demonstrated that the system was governable. The destitution of President Dilma Rousseff in 2016, through an impeachment, brought new issues to the academic world. Although it is clear she has lost considerable legislative support, there is a core issue regarding the role of rules and institutions in determining the problems and the personal management characteristics of President Dilma. This debate is still open and will not be the focus of this issue.

The literature of legislative studies has been developed with the intention of understanding and criticising how governability happens in Brazil, how the Executive and Legislative Branches interact in assembling a government coalition. It has been pursued to answer questions such as what the Legislature's role would be in the development of public policies, its degree of responsivity to electors and the strategies for parliamentary activity. In other terms, it has questioned the quality of this democracy under the perspective of power sharing, of the construction of a public agenda, of dialogue between politicians and society, that is, the intermingling of the Legislature with the quality of democracy in Brazil.

We can see the Legislative Branch in Brazil is a consequence of the national political development, in which the institutional ruptures, the fragility of democracy and the discontinuity in electoral representation hinder its role as a political agent due to a lack of democratic transparency, culture and values, besides the instability of the partisan political scenario. On the other hand, the Legislature is also a cause of the same scenario of limited democratic development, since its action might help to develop democratic elements in Brazil, such as the debate and transparency of public policies. In reference to promoting transparency and public debate, we could question the Legislature's dedication and efficiency.

In theoretical terms, the classic work by N. Polsby (1975) about legislatures provides the key framework for this issue's analysis of the representative linkage facilitated by the Brazilian Chamber of Deputies. Although there are other typologies for legislatures (Blondel, 1970; Mezey, 1979; Morgenstern & Nacif, 2002; Norton, 1984; Packenham, 1970), Polsby's work enlightens the issue of the role of the Legislative Branch in the decision-making process and in political communication, which supports the theme of the articles presented here. Besides that, Polsby's reflection relates the roles performed by the Legislature with its organisational structure, which, in the Brazilian case, is very relevant, since, as previously stated, it is unusually large when compared with the international experience.

Polsby presents a continuum with extremes defined as transformative and arena legislatures. The first one is exemplified by the US Congress and the second one by the UK parliament (both examples based on the author's experience up until the 1970s).[6] The transformative legislature is one that includes the following characteristics: extension and depth in its policy-making actions, enacts its decisions in front of the public, and in a distinguished moment of the action of the Executive Branch, and also encompasses a complex organisational structure. The arena legislature is the one that does not influence much independently in the development of public policies, but shows clearly to the voters who is the government, who is the opposition, and the responsibilities of the government in the performance of public policies, economy, etc. In this perspective, the debate performed in parliament informs public opinion and acts as an educational element for the nation, is strategic to the political actors of the society – since it allows for the identification of the acting political forces – and it also influences the political debate. In order to keep transparency and accountability of the actors, it has a simpler and more intelligible organisational structure.

According to Polsby (1975), transformative legislatures are allegedly more subject to the pressures of the structures and the internal subcultural rules in its actions, while the arena legislatures converse with society in the pattern government–opposition, or, according to Cox (1987), holding the office responsible for the governing action, both in legislative activities and in the implementation of public policies.

The articles of this issue take into consideration, therefore, that the Brazilian Legislative Branch needs to be treated as a very large organisational structure where the number of employees, the volume of the expenses and the diversity of activities performed are significant. We believe these characteristics influence its policy-making and political communication activities. The extent to which this structure allows for acting in the development of public policies is more directly addressed in the first section of articles of the issue. Whereas the second section of the issue concerns several structures related to communication (traditional and digital media) and the contact strategies of the Brazilian Parliament with society, indicating activities that are more related to the arena-type legislatures.

Hence, a question about the Brazilian Congress comes forth. On the one hand, it presents an extensive management structure that privileges the activities of communication and interaction with society, as well as a broad commission system[7] and support structures for the deputies, such as offices and partisan leaderships. On the other hand, its political prerogatives and responsibilities concerning governing activities are, at most, average, if compared with the US Congress. Would this, then, be a transformative legislature, as posed by Polsby (1975), or an arena legislature?

The legislatures of presidentialist systems, a group to which Brazil belongs – except for the US – are allegedly distinguished by their lesser capacity to influence government decisions (Morgenstern & Nacif, 2002), a result of the lower number of institutional prerogatives, of fewer political responsibilities, and of the political dynamics of the countries themselves, in which the Executive Branch is the core element.

Then, another question remains: why is the Chamber of Deputies very large, in structural terms, but does not perform great policy-making or political communication activities in the traditional terms of an arena legislature, as defined by Polsby?

A possible interpretation for the size and organisational complexity of the Brazilian Congress rests in a question: are the activities performed by the Legislative Branch, allegedly, especially those related to the involvement and disclaiming of information, an attempt to compensate for the insufficient political communication actions put forth by the partisan and electoral systems of Brazil? The great number of structures and parallel roles in the Chamber of Deputies for supporting the legislators would allegedly serve to address democratic and representation needs not addressed through the usual avenue of partisan and electoral actions. Despite the need for a sophisticated organisational structure (Griffith & Leston-Bandeira, 2012), the activities performed by the offices and services of the Chamber of Deputies might imply an improvement in the relationship between the parliamentarians and their voters, bringing the society and parliament closer and collaborating to the actualisation of representation.

Thus, the large organisational structure of the Legislative Branch is useful not only to compensate for the loss of power of parliament in the legislating roles of policy-making, but also to set new assignments for the parliamentary organisation, including the symbolic representation posed by Pitkin (Leston-Bandeira, 2012; Pitkin, 1967). A second improvement would be the support of political careers in a broad sense, by emphasising the communication of parliamentary activities and the insertion of the representatives in the political field, that is, in the political elite of the country. After all, as Polsby himself admits, parliaments also have the role of keeping the legitimacy of the system and of recruiting new leaderships.

The first four articles in this issue deal with the legislative role of the Brazilian Legislature, especially with regards to the Executive Branch; while the last two focus on the representative role and on the aspects – contact with citizens and political engagement, for instance – of the Brazilian Parliament that could bring it closer to the concept of arena, according to Polsby's theories.

In the first article, Guimarães, Braga and Miranda[8] explain the historical process of institutionalisation of the Chamber of Deputies, where the institutional ruptures are the core explaining element of the institution's trajectory. The legislative careers and the organisation and internal operations of the Chamber of Deputies are assessed as elements that stimulate or hinder an improved performance regarding transparency and policy-making of the institution.

The second article, by Pinto, brings focuses on the roles and functions of the Brazilian Legislature in a historical and sociological perspective. It presents the changes experienced by the Chamber after the 1988 Constitution and shows how continuity in the process has affected the institution. The author demonstrates that the Legislative Branch continues to play a secondary role when compared with the Executive Branch, a position which it has been forced to share with other political actors.

The subsequent article by Martins and Gomes explores some case studies about the production of laws regarding two key social issues – education and health – in order to analyse in detail the legislative process and the contribution of the Legislature to public policies. On education, the study presents a content analysis of the legislative proposals of parliamentarians and three case studies that discuss policy definitions of funding and quality assessment covering the period of two presidents from opposing parties (Fernando Henrique Cardoso and Luís Inácio Lula da Silva, 1995–2010). On health, the article analyses legislative proposals that resulted in rules for funding. The article suggests that the Congress in Brazil has an important role in defining public policies in these two areas, acting either as a transforming agent or as an arena for debates.

In the same way, the next article, by Schneider and Marques, discusses the behaviour of the Legislature regarding environmental bills from a perspective that takes the roles of the Executive Branch in the Brazilian legislative process into account. Common sense in Brazil tends to consider bills proposed by the Executive as initiatives to protect the environment, while the legislative bias would be to relax legal restrictions on the use of natural resources, thus relegating to Congress the burden of a 'grey' or negative agenda. The article examines all of the environmental bills presented in the Lower House (Chamber of Deputies) and the Upper House (Senate), their goals and approval rate, in order to compare the roles and partialities of the Executive and Legislative Branches in drafting Brazilian environmental acts.

The second part of this issue includes two papers that focus on the relationship between the Brazilian Legislature and society. Barros, Bernardes and Rodrigues examine how new technologies are employed by the Brazilian Chamber of Deputies to stimulate experiences of engagement with parliament, more specifically in the period ranging from the late 1990s to the early 2000s, when the information and publicising system of the House was redesigned, with the advent of new media. The article is theoretically affiliated with engagement and democracy, and assesses how the interactive actions happening now at the Brazilian Parliament can 'shape' the branch as a transformative or arena institution, according to Polsby's (1975) definition.

Specifically regarding digital platforms and technologies, Faria and Rodrigues then present a critical analysis of initiatives for the Open Parliament Policy. Since this policy encompasses two combined fronts, they discuss two sets of practices, one facing the channels of participation in the legislative process, and another focusing on the experiences of Transparency 2.0 (or collaborative transparency). The analysis is theoretically embedded in the discussion about the importance of participation in the current representative systems. In the end, open parliamentary politics are criticised from the perspective of Polsby (1975), assessing the extent to which such mechanisms are close or far from the arena or transformative types of parliament.

Other than considering the Brazilian Parliament as an arena or transformative institution, the articles aim to stimulate a debate about the extent and role of parliaments in presidential systems and countries with heterogeneous and complex political contexts, represented by extreme diversity of interests, beliefs, and social and economic conditions for its populations.

The issue allows us to conclude that the Chamber of Deputies has recently tried to become more active in its relationship with the citizens and in the development of public policies. However, its influence over public policies is still not key. The Chamber of Deputies has also sought to equip itself with services and technologies to reach out to citizens. However, this is a movement that appears to be largely stimulated by the administrative body of the institution, being only partially embraced by actual parliamentarians.

Notes

1. In 1993, a referendum happened and presidentialism was chosen as the preferred method of government by the majority of Brazilians.
2. Legislate, enforce and represent is the motto present in the Constitution of 1988.
3. There are about 30 employees for each parliamentarian in the Chamber of Deputies.
4. Each deputy has an office with equipment (computers, desks, telephones, etc.) and employees chosen by themselves, but paid for by the institution, to perform their activities. Among the resources that are available are airline tickets, funds

for keeping an office in their states, allowances for correspondence, reimburse-ment for fuel, etc.

5. The number oscillates due to constant appointments and discharges. Cf. http://www2.camara.leg.br/transparencia/recursos-humanos/quadro-remuneratorio
6. It is not the goal of this compilation to discuss whether the current configur-ation of the North-American Congress or of the British Parliament still allows for their classification according to Polsby in the extremes. Our point here is the validity of the model in analysing the Brazilian Congress.
7. The Chamber of Deputies currently has 25 permanent commissions, which are responsible for most of the stream of proposals, plus several temporary (ad hoc) commissions.
8. The authors of all the articles are employees at the Chamber of Deputies and faculties at the MA in Legislative Affairs of the Chamber of Deputies, except for Ana A. B. Marques, who is associated to the Legislative Chamber of the Federal District.

Disclosure statement

No potential conflict of interest was reported by the authors.

References

Abranches, S. H. (1988). Presidencialismo de Coalizão: o Dilema Institucional Brasileiro. *Dados: Revista de Ciências Sociais*, Rio de Janeiro. *31*(1), 5–38.
Blondel, J. (1970). Legislative behaviour: Some steps towards a cross-national measurement. *Government and Opposition*, 5(1), 67–85.
Braga, R. J. e Guimarães, A. S. (2015). Um dilema em perspectiva: leituras e releituras do presidencialismo de coalizão. In Sathler, A. e Braga, R. J. (org.), *Legislativo pós-1988: reflexões e perspectivas* (pp. 47–83). Brasília: Edições Câmara.
BRASIL. IBGE. Instituto Brasileiro de Geografia e Estatística. (2016). *IBGE divulga as estimativas populacionais dos municípios em 2016*. [IBGE publishes population's

estimation of cities in 2016.]. Retrieved from http://saladeimprensa.ibge.gov.br/noticias?view=noticia&id=1&idnoticia=3244&busca=1

Cox, G. W. (1987). *The efficient secret: The cabinet and the development of political parties in Victorian England.* Cambridge: Cambridge University Press.

Figueiredo, A. C., & Limongi, F. (1995). Mudança Constitucional, Desempenho do Legislativo e Consolidação Institucional. *Revista Brasileira de Ciências Sociais,* N. *29*(ano 10), 175–200.

Figueiredo, A. C., & Limongi, F. (1997). O *Congresso e as Medidas Provisórias*: Abdicação ou Delegação. *Novos Estudos CEBRAP, 47,* 127–154.

Figueiredo, A. C., & Limongi, F. (2001). *Executivo e Legislativo na Nova Ordem Constitucional* (2ª ed.). Rio de Janeiro: FGV.

Figueiredo, A. C., & Limongi, F. (2008). *Política Orçamentária no Presidencialismo de Coalizão.* Rio de Janeiro: FGV.

Figueiredo, A. C., Limongi, F., & Valente, A. L. (1999). Governabilidade e concentração de poder institucional – o Governo FHC. *Tempo Social,* USP, S. Paulo, *11*(2), 49–62.

Freyre, G. (2001). *Casa-grande & senzala.* Rio de Janeiro: Record. (Introdução à história da sociedade patriarcal no Brasil: 1).

Furtado, C. (2008). *Formação econômica do Brasil.* São Paulo: Companhia das Letras.

Griffith, J., & Leston-Bandeira, C. (2012). How are parliaments using new media to engage with citizens? *The Journal of Legislative Studies, 18*(3–4), 496–513. doi:10.1080/13572334.2012.706058

Guimarães, A. S., Schwartz, F. P., Souza, J. W., & Melo, M. R. M. (2015). Strategic management in legislative public management: A comparative perspective. *International Business and Management, 11,* 13–24.

Ianni, O. (1978). O *colapso do populismo no Brasil* (4ª ed.). Rio de Janeiro: Civilização Brasileira.

Leston-Bandeira, C. (2012). Parliaments' endless pursuit of trust: Re-focusing on symbolic representation. *The Journal of Legislative Studies, 18*(3–4), 514–526.

Limongi, F., & Figueiredo, A. C. (1998). Bases Institucionais do Presidencialismo de Coalizão. *Lua Nova – Revista de Cultura e Política, 44,* 81–106.

Linz, J. J. (1994). Presidential or parliamentary democracy: Does it make a difference? In J. J. Linz & A. Valenzuela (Eds.), *The failure of presidential democracy: The case of Latin America* (pp. 18–26). Baltimore: J. Hopkins Univ. Press.

Llanos, M., & Nolte, D. (2003). Bicameralism in the americas: Around the extremes of symmetry and incongruence. *The Journal of Legislative Studies, 9*(3), 54–86.

Marenco, A. (2007). Devagar se vai ao longe? In Melo, Carlos Ranulfo, Alcántara Sáez, Manuel (Orgs.), *A Democracia Brasileira: Balanço e perspectivas para o século 21* (pp. 73–105). Belo Horizonte: UFMG.

Medeiros, V. A. S., *et al.* (2011). *A Política do Espaço*: Uma Investigação Comparativa entre a Estrutura Espacial e o Desempenho das Atividades em Casas Legislativas (Congresso Nacional/Brasil e Assembleia da República/Portugal). Projeto de Grupo de Pesquisa. Câmara dos Deputados, 2011.

Mezey, M. (1979). *Comparative legislatures.* Durham, NC: Duke University Press.

Morgenstern, S., & Nacif, B. (2002). *Legislative politics in Latin America.* Cambridge, NY: Cambridge University Press. (Cambridge studies in comparative politics).

Norton, P. (1984). Parliament and policy in Britain: The House of Commons as a policy influencer. *Teaching Politics, 13,* 198–221.

Packenham, R. (1970). Legislatures and political development. In A. Kornberg & L. Musolf (Eds.), *Legislatures in developmental perspective* (pp. 521–582). Durham, NC: Durham University Press.

Palermo, V. (2000). *Como se governa o Brasil?* [electronic resource]: O debate sobre instituições políticas e gestão de governo. Rio de Janeiro: Instituto Universitário de Pesquisas do Rio de Janeiro.

Pires, J. M. (2011). A *Implantação da Representação Proporcional de Lista Aberta no Brasil*. 2011. In Nicolau, J., & Braga, R. J. (Eds.), *Para Além das Urnas: reflexões sobre a Câmara dos Deputados* (pp. 21–44). Brasília: Edições Câmara.

Pitkin, H. F. (1967). *The concept of representation*. Berkeley: University of Califórnia.

Polsby, N. (1975). Legislatures. In F. I. Greenstein & N. W. Polsby (Eds.), *Handbook of political science, V* (pp. 257–319). Reading, MA: Addison-Wesley.

Porto, W. C. (2002). *O Voto no Brasil: da Colônia à 6ª República* (2ª ed.). Rio de Janeiro: Top Books.

Power, T. J. (2015). *Presidencialismo de coalizão e o design institucional no Brasil*: o que sabemos até agora? In Sathler, A. e Braga, R. J. (org), *Legislativo pós-1988: reflexões e perspectivas* (pp. 15–45). Brasília: Edições Câmara.

Prado Jr, C. (1970). *História econômica do Brasil*. São Paulo: Brasiliense.

Renno, L. R. (2006). Críticas ao Presidencialismo de Coalizão no Brasil: Processos Institucionalmente Constritos ou Individualmente Dirigidos? In L. Avritzer, & F. Anastasia (Org.), *Reforma Política no Brasil* (pp. 259–271). Belo Horizonte: Editora da UFMG.

Santos, W. G. (1986). *Sessenta e Quatro*: Anatomia da Crise. São Paulo: Vértice.

Weffort, F. (1980). *O Populismo na política brasileira*. Rio de Janeiro: Paz e Terra.

The institutionalisation of the Brazilian Chamber of Deputies

Ricardo de João Braga, André Rehbein Sathler and Roberto Campos da Rocha Miranda

ABSTRACT
This article analyses the institutional development of the Brazilian Chamber of Deputies (BCD) from 1826 to the present. Legislature careers, the internal organisation of the BCD, the current system for filling positions within the committees and electoral rules are the objects of this study. The process of development of the BCD should be understood in light of the dynamics of the Brazilian political system, which has undergone significant ruptures of regime, and also in light of the nearly permanent fragility of the democracy, especially of its representative components. It is an institution with legislature career patterns that vary through time, but always point towards opportunities out of the BCD, a stable, hierarchical and complex mode of organisation that currently values parties as distributors of opportunities. It is, above all, an institution that is subject to external influences from other parts of the political system, which diminish its autonomy and self-determination, as shown by the example of the rule for the adjudication of terms. With its 190 years, the BCD has evolved along with Brazilian democracy and today, although boasting a great structure and large resources, it still needs to establish itself as a decisive and permanent actor in driving public policies and communication (parties and government projects) with voters.

Introduction

The Brazilian Chamber of Deputies (BCD) initiated its activities in 1826, four years after the independence of Brazil. This article aims to analyse its institutionalisation process, as seen in the development of its political and organisational structure, its ability for action, its autonomy, and specialisation.

The BCD is the lower chamber of the Brazilian National Legislative Branch. After the independence of Brazil, a constitutional monarchic system was established, with a unitary state and a bicameral Legislative Branch, comprised of a Chamber of Deputies and a Senate. At first the system was controlled by the Emperor, D. Pedro I. When he went back to Portugal in 1831, to take over the Portuguese throne, Brazil started being ruled by regents. In 1840 D. Pedro II took over the throne, and a type of

16

parliamentarianism was established in 1847 (Chacon, 2007) with a Minister Cabinet stemming from the Legislative Branch and appointed by the Emperor. This system would remain until 1889, when the monarchy was deposed and a presidential republic was established, inspired by the example of the United States of America.

During the Empire, the members of the BCD were elected by a two-tier majority system (with property qualification), for fixed terms, and the BCD could be dissolved by the Emperor. The Senate was tenured, appointed by the Emperor and the main components of the Minister's Cabinet came from its ranks.

In the republican period, the Brazilian State became federal, senators started being elected and the property qualification for elections was dropped. From then on, a presidential system was established, with fixed terms for the Legislative and the Executive Branches and without re-election for the Executive Branch (one consecutive re-election started being allowed for the Executive Branch from 1999 onwards). The electoral system for deputies was still based on a majority criterion, being changed to proportional in 1932 (Pires, 2011). From independence to 1930, the Brazilian electoral process was considered fraudulent in all its steps: registering, qualification of voters, voting, counting, verification, and recognition of diplomas. The word of order of the ongoing efforts for reforming the system was 'electoral truth', a goal that was never reached (Porto, 2002). After 1945, Brazil reached a new level. Considering the democratic characterisation of Dahl (1997), Brazil started to meet better the criteria for competitive elections, plurality and participation.

During the republican period there were ruptures of democracy, such as the *coup d'état* by Getúlio Vargas in 1930, followed by a dictatorship from 1937 to 1945, and the military regime from 1964 to 1985, periods during which the Legislative Branch underwent deep changes, especially the violation of legislative careers, loss of prerogatives and even the interruption of its activities. The redemocratisation periods, on the contrary, retrieved the prerogatives of the Legislative Branch.

The twentieth century, especially after 1930, was the period where the masses started to participate in politics under the modern democratic logic of participation, voting and public opinion. The political parties gained national range after 1945 – since the beginning of the Republic they had been state-bound and during the Empire they had little social penetration (Benevides, 1981, 1989; Fleischer, 2007; Hippolito, 1985; Carvalho, 1996). With the military regime, bipartisanship was imposed (1966–79), and afterwards, a multi-party system was re-established.

The development of the BCD and its analysis, therefore, are related to the evolution of the Brazilian political system in its wider dimension, by following the great movements of rupture of regimes and structural changes in politics.

In theoretical terms, this article uses, as its basis of concepts, method and comparative data about institutionalisation, the works of Polsby (1968), Hibbing (1988) and Opello (1986), and also dialogues with the legislative classification of Polsby (1975).

The analysis of the institutionalisation aims to verify to which measure the BCD was able to become a permanent, well-defined political entity that is distinguished from the other entities of the system. The BCD was never set up as the centre of the political power of the nation, but that is not necessary to characterise its institutionalisation. In fact, the centre of power has always been the Executive Branch, be it during the Empire or during the presidential republic.

What is remarkable about the Legislative Branch is its almost uninterrupted presence since 1826, the permanence of the bicameral structure, and the stability of its internal organisation. Throughout time, the BCD has grown in its volume of resources and today it is an enormous organisation, with approximately 15,000 employees for a total of 513 deputies, a ratio of approximately 30 employees per representative, well above the global standards (Guimarães, Schwartz, Souza, & Melo, 2015), and with a budget that surpasses US$ 1 billion per year.[1]

This article is separated into three sections, besides the Introduction and Conclusion. The first one is about the career of the federal deputies in a historical perspective, in which the gauging of seniority and career standards are emphasised. The second section concerns the structure and the organisational design, with an emphasis on the description of the organisational evolution of the BCD since its creation. The third section deals with the advance of universal and impersonal rules, specifically the rules for the assumption of positions in the committees and the mechanisms for certifying electoral results (rule adjudication).

Legislative careers

Regarding political organisations, Polsby (1968) associates the establishment of its limits with the restriction of career opportunities. He presumes that, in the absence of an institutionalisation process, the members come and go easily, rising to leadership is easy, and temporal stability in leadership becomes rare.

Inspired by Polsby (1968), the present study analyses the following data: (1) percentage of first term members[2] for each legislature; (2) average number of terms for each legislature; (3) years of term before the first selection for president; and (4) later activities of the president (years and final position).[3] Regarding the number of novice members in the BCD, the situation is as described in Figure 1.

The entry of novices oscillates between approximately 20 and 80 per cent. There is no monotonic evolution during the entire period, but sub-periods

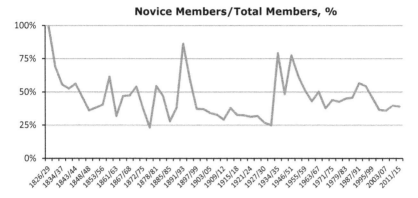

Figure 1. Amount of novice members (%). Source: Chamber of Deputies. Created by the authors.

and ruptures, when the number of novices grows after a few institutional ruptures. Regarding the sub-periods, we have a standard of oscillation during the Empire and another more stable period with the First Republic, until 1930. The Vargas years are atypical (1930–45). The post-Vargas redemocratisation, the military regime (1964–85) and the post-military redemocratisation (post-1985) encompass a rather stable period, without any deep ruptures, except for a lower stability after 1994.

During the Empire, the great oscillation in the number of novices may have been caused by the alternation of the parties in power, Conservative and Liberal (we do not have any data about the affiliation of deputies to verify the hypothesis). As pointed out by a few analysts (Porto, 2002), the Brazilian system worked from the top to the bottom. Curiously, first the Emperor nominated the Minister Cabinet, and only then called for elections. Therefore, the elections were just a means to legitimise the Cabinet.[4] These dynamics that were commanded from the top, as well as a possible discouragement of legislative careers, may explain the frequent peaks in the number of novices during the Empire. A great rupture happened with the fall of the Empire and the beginning of the Republic, which can be attributed to the new political standard that was implemented (with new parties and the end of the tenured Senate) and the refusal of advocates of the monarchy to participate in the new system.

The First Republic (1889–1930), with a liberal character, consolidated and established the state oligarchies and was supported by them (local groups were established and each state was represented by a local majority party). Representation in the BCD thus mirrors the stable political tableau. Only in 1930, with the rupture of the entire political system, do we see changes in the standard of the BCD.

From 1930 to 1945 Getúlio Vargas promoted changes that weakened federalism and extinguished state parties, as well as closing the Congress and suspending elections from 1938 to 1945. The only period with political-partisan activities was between 1933 and 1937 (Fleischer, 2007, p. 304). These actions broke the pattern of political disputes and interrupted legislative careers. Thus, the Vargas period of power characterises a short and specific moment for the BCD. With the redemocratisation in 1945, another phase began, which continues today.

We understand that the only reason for there being only one legislative career period after 1945 is because the military *coup d'état* altered the election system more for the Executive Branch positions and less for the BCD, which allowed for a reasonable degree of continuity in the careers of deputies. The militaries took the president of the Republic away from his position of power in 1964, but held the legislative and state government elections (State Executive Branch) in 1965 and the partisan structure that already existed until 1966 (from 1966 onwards the elections for governors and mayors of big cities became indirect). The largest impact in the BCD was the forfeiture of parliamentarians (67 deputies between 1964 and 1966 (Braga, 2014), in a total of 287 positions in the Lower Chamber). The extinction of the multi-party system in 1966 saw a return to a two-party system of situation and opposition (Fleischer, 2007), which in a certain way only reaccommodated the political forces and the politicians that survived the forfeitures of the beginning of the regime.

Although the *coup d'état* was very deep in many aspects of political life, the military regime installed made the choice of maintaining legislative elections practically unchanged during the entire period, which did not increase the rate of novices, and, thus, did not constitute a proper rupture. Consequentially, the current period of redemocratisation, especially the 1980s, did not present renovation trends that deviated from a historical average. Regarding the number of novices and legislative careers, we observe a reasonable continuity from 1945 until today. The military regime did not cause deep ruptures like the beginning of the Republic or the Vargas coup.

The consequence of the renovation rate is observable in Figure 2, which shows the average of terms carried out by the deputies of each legislature. There are three somewhat distinguished blocks. The first block shows the Empire BCD, the second shows the First Republic (from 1891 to 1930), and the third one encompasses the democratic period between 1945 and 1964, the military regime and the beginning of the redemocratisation (until 1994), with a sub-period that began in 1995.

The three specified periods reflect specialisation and solidification movements of political careers within the BCD. The government experience of the Empire is somewhat homogeneous and the number of terms of the parliamentarians, in a crescent trend during the period, demonstrates how the political class specialised in parliamentary activities. The beginning of the Republic (1889–1930) controlled by local state elites is the period with the largest

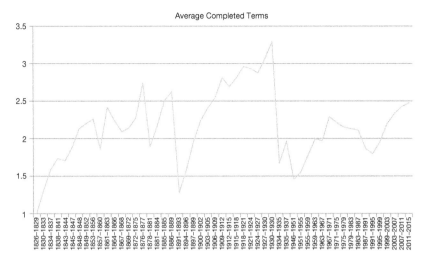

Figure 2. Average of completed terms. Source: Chamber of Deputies. Created by the authors.

permanence and stability of parliamentarians in the BCD. From 1945 to the present, including two democratic periods and one dictatorship, we see a political group that underwent two transitions, entering and leaving an exceptional context. The nature of the Brazilian military dictatorship, one of the least disruptive ones in Latin America, somewhat consociative and presenting longer transitions (Marenco, 2007), explains how this parliamentary elite was able to mature in the Congress even before apparently disruptive factors.

We understand there is a pattern for novices only post-1945, but there is a sub-period of greater specialisation after 1994. Besides the direct reading of data, this is explained by the fact that, after 1995, a period of greater governing stability begins, marked especially by the Fernando Henrique Cardoso and Lula-Dilma administrations, during which the polarisation of the system between PSDB (Brazilian Social Democracy Party) and PT (Worker's Party) (both supported by parties with very low ideological and programmatic consistency, such as PMDB, PP, PTB, etc.) lent more stability to the electoral competition. The number of novices (Figure 1) dropped a little bit after 1994 and became primarily stable in this pattern, which forced the average of terms completed to rise clearly after this date (Figure 2).

We can affirm that, within each period, the BCD saw a potential growth in the capacity of its constituents, considered especially from their experience in the position. However, we emphasise that the average of completed terms rarely surpasses 2.5, which means something between seven and 10 years of term, which does not amount to much experience for a parliamentarian. The average number of terms is also related to the limits of the political system. The Brazilian case shows that, in each of the periods referred to,

21

the branches of power started to create barriers, but some ruptures were disruptive and dismantled patterns that were being built.

Another issue related to legislative careers concerns the intentions of the parliamentarians. For the current period, most of the literature (cf. note 3) considers that the career goal of parliamentarians is, in particular, obtaining positions in the Executive Branch, especially as mayors and governors. Thus, even during periods of institutional stability, the call for careers out of the Legislative Branch is seductive and removes the most ambitious and key figures from the BCD.

Another face of the attraction of legislative careers, of the specialisation and the importance of the BCD, is shown in Figure 3, which presents the time (in years) between their first election for the BCD and the moment they are elected president of the House.

Once more, there is no clear pattern of fall or growth. The linear trend is growing but is probably influenced by the beginning of the period, with necessarily low values (a mobile average of 10 periods, on the other hand, demonstrates only an oscillation, with no apparent trend). Except for the first legislature, there are four cases of presidents who were elected as soon as they took office: 1834, a very incipient legislature; 1864, on the shift of a long-living conservative office to a liberal one:[5] 1891 and 1946, these two linked to moments of institutional rupture.

We can affirm that the BCD has not demanded a growing experience from those who reached its presidency. There are senior and novice

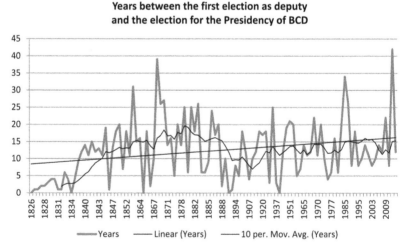

Years between the first election as deputy and the election for the Presidency of BCD

Years ——— Linear (Years) ——— 10 per. Mov. Avg. (Years)

Figure 3. Years between the first election for BCD and election for presidency. Source: Chamber of Deputies. Created by the authors.

Note: Only one election was considered, the first one, when the president was consecutively re-elected. Non-consecutive re-elections were computed.

parliamentarians that rose to presidency in all its periods. We must consider that the political dynamics of the Empire, a period during which many highly majoritarian compositions of BCD existed (Porto, 2002), oscillating between conservatives and liberals, caused constant renewals of the BCD, for the composition of the Assembly suffered great alternation of parties. Regarding the current period, there are rules that stop the president of the BCD maintaining the position from the first half of their legislature into the second half of their term. In the USA (Polsby, 1968) there are presidents who held the chair of the presidency of the House of Representatives for a long time. This, however, is not the Brazilian standard, both for electoral reasons – which change the composition of the Assembly, creating new majorities – and for regulatory reasons (obstruction to re-election in the same legislature, since the 1970s).

Tables 1 and 2 add up information to these dynamics of the parliamentary career, enabling the comprehension of the goals of those who reach the presidency of the BCD. The continuity of the career enables the comprehension of their goals, which may be out of the BCD.

Table 3 show several important characteristics of the institutionalisation of the BCD. First, the period of the public activity of the presidents after leaving the presidency is very high. The average varies between a minimum of 11.5 years and a maximum of 22.6 years, depending on the historic period. This shows that the position of president of the BCD is not usually the final moment of a political career in Brazil. In fact, only 10 Brazilian politicians in all of its history ended their public careers in this position, from a total of 77 politicians that held the chair of president of the BCD. The position was more important during the first period of the Republic, from 1889 to 1930, since five of the 12 presidents of the BCD during this period ended their career in this position.

The position of senator at the beginning of the Republic and also during the Empire was the most frequent final position. During the Empire, the position of senator was tenured and distinguished the climax of a successful political career. Many of these senators were also presidents of the Minister's Cabinet, the de facto prime minister of the parliamentary system

Table 1. Years of public activity after leaving the presidency of the BCD.

	Empire	1889–1930	1930–37	Post-1945	Post-1945*
Maximum	49	34	29	38	38
Minimum	0	1	9	0	1
Average	22.26	11.50	19.00	16.27	19.71
Standard deviation	11.35	11.94	14.14	10.92	10.98
N	42	12	2	30	21

Source: Created by the authors. Note: For deceased parliamentarians, the difference between the date of death and the date of departure of the presidency of the Chamber was considered; for alive parliamentarians we considered the year of 2015, minus the date they left the presidency of the BCD.
*Excluding active politicians.

Table 2. Political bodies of the BCD considered in the counting.

Included	Excluded*
Presidency	Temporary committees (inquiry, special, general, external and miscellaneous)
Board	Partisan leaderships
Four secretariats	Leader College**
Permanent committees	
Internal police	
Parliamentary Prosecutor	
Women's Office	
Commission's secretariats	

*The bodies were excluded due to their transitory existence (committees) or to the non-identification as regulatory and formally existent bodies in the organisational structure of the BCD.

**The Leader College is a collegiate (created in 1989), but functions in a dissimilar manner from what is advised by the RI (Figueiredo, 2012).

implemented after 1847 (Chacon, 2007, p. 19). During the Empire, 19 of the BCD presidents ended their public lives as senators, and all throughout the Brazilian political history (excluding currently active politicians), 26 of 77 also ended their careers as senators. This fact unveils another characteristic of the Brazilian political system, that is: the Senate was the prevalent House, status-wise, when compared with the BCD, during both the Empire and the Republic. In the current context, the Federal Senate holds more legislative prerogatives than the BCD, contrasting with most of the global legislative experiences (Massicotte, 2001; Llanos & Nolte, 2003; Rogers, 2003; Shell, 2001; Vatter, 2005).

The position of deputy, not the presidency, of the BCD gains in importance only post-1945, when seven of the BCD presidents, from 21, ended their careers in the same House. It is worthwhile to highlight those who ended their careers as presidents of the Republic (three during the period). In all of the three cases (two during the democratic period and the third one

Table 3. Last political position of the president of the BCD.

	Empire	1889–1930	1930–37	Post-1945*	Total
President of the BCD	4	5	1		10
Federal Deputy		1		7	8
Senator	19	5		2	26
Minister of the Executive Branch	9			2	11
President of the Republic				3	3
Vice-president of the Republic			1		1
Positions in the judiciary Branch – budget courts	4			3	7
High positions in public administration/ Executive		1		2	3
Ambassador				2	2
Church	3				3
Others	3				3
Total:	42	12	2	21	77

Source: Created by the authors.

*Excluding active politicians.

during the military regime), the presidency was only reached as a consequence of the vacancy of the position of president of the Republic, following the institutional successive line, in which the president of the BCD is the third, right after the president of the Republic and its vice-president. Thus, we see that, for these three cases, the career in the BCD had, in a certain way, its climax with the presidency of the Lower Chamber, since the presidency of the Republic occurred due to their ascension within the BCD.

We cannot affirm, however, that the BCD has consolidated itself over time as a first-rate political instance. During the different periods of Brazilian history, other positions and arenas competed with it for the privileged position. This career standard corroborates the idea that the BCD is not a very powerful gubernatorial instance (as the Minister Board was during the Empire parliamentarianism and the Executive positions were during the Republic), which reduces its attraction. For the current period (cf. note 3), the literature affirms that the legislative careers follow a pattern of searching for better opportunities in the Executive, and the Legislative Branch is a preparatory instance or a support for other possibilities. If the BCD is not the final destination of a political career, this reduces the incentives for its institutional strengthening.

Organisational stability of the BCD

The internal complexity of a political institution, according to Polsby (1968), is measured by: internal separation of the roles under some sort of regular and explicit basis, non-interchangeability and a degree of interdependence between the parts. The author admits, an opinion shared by Hibbing (1988), that the indexes to measure internal complexity are the most difficult to obtain and the ones that more certainly need to be viewed from the singular reality of each country.

The first important point for the Brazilian case is the prevalence of written regulations (internal regulations, 'by-laws' – RIs), which determine the rights and obligations of the parliamentarians, legislative procedures, the bodies that form the BCD, and its prerogatives. The activities of the legislators are based on the set rules and their interpretations the entire time. Habit, consensus or any other practical action must submit, ultimately, to the RIs. The RIs, in turn, are rules set by the BCD in unicameral procedures, and the Supreme Federal Court (Supremo Tribunal Federal (STF)), the Brazilian Constitutional Court, is exempt from evaluating the provisions and interpretations of the RIs, since it considers this theme to be *interna corporis* (the STF only discusses legislative actions that are explicitly supported by the Federal Constitution).

Since 1826 the BCD has been subject to several RIs: 1826, 1831 (with changes in 1874), 1899, 1904, 1915, 1921, 1928, 1946, 1949, 1972 and 1989 (with changes until the present).

In order to identify and analyse the structure and the operation of the BCD throughout its history, we attempted to identify its political bodies. The method we used was one of nominal equivalence,[6] that is, the proof of permanence of an organ in the structure is its denomination and not the analysis of its competencies. Competency analyses are intuitively attractive and may be significant, but they are also subject to criticism, and less safe due to the subjectivity of their classification, and were, therefore, discarded.

The RIs reveal as structural bodies the presidency (and vice-presidencies), the board, the secretariats (from first to fourth secretary) and the committees (permanent or temporary), leaving to their own regulation the definition of the administrative structure. This allows us to infer that the main concern of the legislator lies in political activities, enabling the shaping of the administrative structure to this context. This finding supports a contemporary organisational characteristic of the BCD that seems to originate in the past: the separation (functional specialisation) between the legislative and administrative sectors (Miranda, 2012).

The counting of the political bodies of the Chamber of Deputies followed the data presented in Table 4.

Generally speaking, we can see a conservation of a directive structure during the evolution of the BCD (presidency, board and secretariats), and a limited variation in the number of committees. We have emphasised the changes in classification and merger of themes in the committees; there are 99 different committee names in the RIs (up to 2015). The separations and mergers in the themes probably occur because of the social context of the time, and returns to committee names from previous periods are occurring in more recent RIs. A novelty when compared with permanent committees is a rise in its number during the life of the 1989 RI (there were 13 in 1989, 19 in 2003 and 24 in 2016).

Table 4. Total of political bodies of the Chamber of Deputies identified in the internal regulations.

Years	Number of bodies
1826	5
1831	26
1874*	28
1899	21
1904	20
1915	21
1921	20
1928	19
1946	9
1949	21
1972	25
1989	24
2014**	35

Source: Created by the authors.
Note: *Change; **Change (13th version, of 2014).

We can see that the number of political bodies is higher, between 20 and 30, with a mode and a mean of 21 bodies. There are three outliers: five (1826, first RI), nine (1946, regulation for the Constitutional Assembly – democratic restoration) and 35 (1989 RI, with a review in 2014, when the committees were broadened and changed).

The more frequent structures of the RIs may be identified in Table 5.

The BCD has never undergone an organic and significant process of change of its organisation. Practically in the second point of the series (1831) we can already see a standard configuration, maintained with few changes throughout the next 180 years. In regard to its power structure, the initial configuration remains almost unaffected: the board (collegiate of president, vice-president and secretaries, with defined and hierarchical attributions) is the main governance body of the BCD. The structure of the board has remained identical since 1831, even though the country has undergone several moments of institutional ruptures. We can think of this process as a institutionalisation through by a normative-traditional way, differently from what was identified in the processes of the North American Chamber of Deputies and the British House of Commons, where we can see an institutionalisation through the consolidation of centenary practices, through a slow process of retreats and advances by means of affirmation of precedents. In the Brazilian case, the initial normative structure was never challenged.

The BCD is subject to a vertical control, with a small supreme collegiate at its summit. There is, therefore, a permanent tension in representation for the Legislative Branch, in principle constituted by a horizontal equality among all of the parliamentarians, but subject to a vertical configuration that aims to centralise procedures and decisions. This limits the possibilities of actions of the parliamentarians at an individual level. During periods of multi-party systems in Brazil (1946–66 and post-1979), the direction also included in its positions the diversity of compositions of the BCD, in a proportional manner related to the importance of each party. As a result of that, in the usual configuration of the BCD throughout history, including its current configuration, the party leaders and board members are the great holders of opportunities within the political process. The backbenchers simply line up to the higher determinations, coming either from their parties or from the political administration of the BCD.

With nine nominations, the Secretariat (an administrative body that does not mix with the director board secretaries, which are political positions) is identified in the RIs, but without displaying its constitutional structure; its activities are related to the administrative issues of the House.

The 2014 version of the RI (Brasil, 2014) is the one with more rules concerning administrative subjects, for it deals with policies and general guidelines to be adopted, without, however, going further into the administrative structure that supports the activities defined. This appearance of the

Table 5. Bodies/structures that show up the most in Rls.

Bodies	Year													Frequency
	1826	1831	1874*	1899	1904	1915	1921	1928	1946	1949	1972	1989	2014**	
Presidency	x	x	x	x	x	x	x	x	x	x	x	x	x	13
Vice-presidency (vice-presidents)	x	x	x	x	x	x	x	x	x	x	x	x	x	13
Board		x	x	x	x	x	x	x	x	x	x	x	x	12
1st Secretariat		x	x	x	x	x	x	x	x	x	x	x	x	12
2nd Secretariat		x	x	x	x	x	x	x	x	x	x	x	x	12
3rd Secretariat		x	x	x	x	x	x	x	x	x	x	x	x	12
4th Secretariat		x	x	x	x	x	x	x	x	x	x	x	x	12
Secretariat	x				x	x	x	x	x	x	x	x		9
Committee for Drafting (of Laws)		x	x	x	x	x	x	x			x	x		9
Maritime and War Commission		x	x	x	x	x	x	x						7
House Police Committee (of the House)		x	x	x	x	x	x	x						7
Public Health Commission		x	x		x	x	x	x		x				7
Instruction (Public) Commission		x	x		x	x	x	x						6
Constitution and Justice Commission					x	x	x	x			x	x		6
Finance Commission					x	x	x	x		x	x			6
Committee of Diplomacy and Treaties				x		x	x	x			x			5
Committee for Accounts					x	x	x	x		x				5

Source: Created by the authors, based on Bylaws of the Chamber of Deputies (Brasil, 1826, 1832/1931, 1874, 1899, 1904, 1915, 1921, 1928, 1946, 1949, 1972, 1989/2011, 2014).
Note: *Change; **Change (13th version, of 2014).

regulation of administrative activities happened at the end of a process during which the BCD spread out into a wide structure with 15,000 employees and was spending more than R$ 5 billion/year.

In regards to specialisation, taking the committees as a basis, we verify that some themes are the object of constant attention: education is dealt with since 1831; communications arise in the 1904 RI and remain; and health has been a focus of committees since 1831. On the other hand, some bodies are granted more relevance according to the historic context, such as the 'committee for colonisation and civilisation of Indians', present in the RI of 1826 and extinct in 1904.

The permanence, more than the changes, is characteristics of the organisation of the BCD. This fact hypothetically points to two fronts. The first one regards the dynamics of the Brazilian political process that seems to isolate the BCD from external checks, creating a context of low accountability and compromise with gubernatorial activities.

Brazil was never rooted in democracy, with strong representative practices, both in the liberal and participant senses. On the other hand, clientelism and patrimonialism are endemic (Nunes, 2010). Thus, a body with a stable format, that only grows in size over time (employs more people, spends more money) is coherent with low democratic response dynamics, technocratic insulation, clientelism and patrimonialism (Faoro, 2009; Nunes, 2010; Souza, 1990).

The second point refers to a valorisation of legal-formal models in politics, something that adheres to the Ibero-Brazilian tradition of *bacharelismo* (valorisation of the form of the rule, of legal careers, of classic rhetoric, etc.) and a tendency to copy foreign institutions. We can affirm that the structure of the BCD includes specialised, permanent and somewhat autonomous bodies, since the committees have presented since their inception a stable aspect and division of work, as well as its directive bodies, the board and its components.

We conclude with regards to the internal complexity of the BCD that it is stable, having been defined in its first moments, during the Empire. For some scholars, the bicameral imperial model was influenced by the English (Chacon, 2007), and the Republic model was influenced by the North Americans (Porto, 2002). In any case, as we have already pointed out, it is not a native construction or a model that was organically built, based on internal issues and establishment of precedents. It is much more the assumption of a foreign model that is stabilised due to a certain insulation and lack of responsiveness of the institution in regard to the *demos*. We could therefore infer that, to some extent, this model meets the interests of the forces that alternate in leading the BCD, forces that are typical of a historically oligarchic country.

In addition to the patterns of legislative career, which do not favour the BCD, and do not generate expertise and investment of the parliamentarians in the institution, with the characteristics of the structure – hierarchical, centralised, stable – we cannot univocally define the BCD as a transformative or arena legislative (Polsby, 1975), for example. We should take into account that a structure with a collegiate directive body and dispersion in several committees, combined with a proportional electoral system (and a multiparty background – functioning during the democratic periods since 1945), hinders the perception by the citizens of the forces that are responsible for governing the country. The prerogatives and responsibilities are apparently diffused among the different bodies, parties and parliamentarians (and this lack of identification is the opposite of what is expected of an arena legislative branch).[7]

On the other hand, we are not talking about a univocally transformative legislature. A transformative legislature, although its sophisticated internal division of tasks (mirroring political bodies), such as the BCD, also has other attributes. First, it demands expertise from its legislators, which was demonstrated in the previous section not to be true. Still, it depends on the prerogatives of the BCD themselves. Although they have not been deeply analysed in this article,[8] we can see that the BCD was never prevalent in the determination of public policies. The Executive Branch in Brazil, with the Minister Cabinet in the Empire, and later the president of the Republic, have always had more prerogatives in terms of formulation and implementation of public policies.

Universality of rules: external forces and internal changes to the BCD

The prevalence of universal rules and automatic decisions constitutes an element of institutionalisation. To the agents involved, it diminishes risk and uncertainty in the decision-making process, and to the citizens it represents an increment in the quality of representation, since political actions are less affected by casuistry. Polsby (1968) seeks to identify the phenomenon in the valorisation of seniority as a criterion for accessing positions in the legislative committees and merit as a criterion to decide on controversial elections.

The BCD committees, especially today, are not gatekeepers of their themes. Although they participate in the treatment of the themes, their exclusivity might be bypassed by the direct submission of propositions to the floor, which happens by request of the party leaders, or when the deadline for appreciation of propositions urgently submitted by the Executive Branch has passed. Still, in Brazil, the committee most aligned with the proposition does not have any exclusivity over its analysis, quite the opposite: all of the committees that are linked to the theme have the right to evaluate it, and when more than three committees have that right, an ad hoc committee is created (where not all members need to be in the original committees) and the original committees are excluded from the evaluation.

Nonetheless, the positions in the BCD committees are fought for, because they represent opportunities and resources for a political career. There are more and less important committees, depending on the number of propositions they appreciate and on the evaluated theme. Positions in committees generate opportunities for speech and more immediate participation in deliberations. The committee presidents can also appoint a number of employees, which is an important power resource in Brazil (clientelism).

In the BCD, the filling of positions in the legislative committee currently does not follow any universal criteria. The committee chairs are distributed to each party according to their proportional size on the floor, and the leader appoints their representatives. Regarding the presidencies of the collegiate, they are also proportionally distributed to the party (Aguiar, 2015). Thus, the distribution of opportunities is contextual, depending on the strength of the party and also on the strength of the specific parliamentarian in the party, which does not contribute to the stability of the membership and also diminishes the possibilities of expertise and action of the committee, since a reasonable turnover in its composition is generated.

Seniority is not a relevant criterion to appoint positions: there are cases where novice politicians in the BCD obtain privileged positions in committees and even the presidency, because of their power within their party. We can affirm that there is no property right of the parliamentarian over the chairs in committee and there is less so a universal set of rules and automation. The values at stake are distributed according to parties and the party leader plays a decisive role in this process, appointing members to the committees and also removing them, at any time.

We should also emphasise that this is the current scenario, in which the re-election of a deputy for the position of committee president is not allowed (the term comprises only a year, and consecutive election has been forbidden since 1972). The consequence of this hindrance is a lack of expertise in the committees, and the cause seems to be a wish – that can also be said of the members of the board, which cannot be re-elected – to spread the opportunities for access to the ruling positions (which is the flip side of the marked difference between the politicians who are in ruling positions and the backbenchers). Sometimes important politicians choose their position in a certain committee because they will hold its presidency, and, in the following year, when they leave their position, they migrate to another committee, a procedure that weakens collegiate.

The composition of committees and the distribution of opportunity between them demonstrate the importance of the parties, which are characteristics that are dissimilar to the findings of Polsby (1968) in the House of Representatives, but approximate the Brazilian scenario to partisan regimes in Europe, for example. The importance of partisan determinations also applies to other bodies of the BCD, such as access to positions on the board and other political structure bodies (such as the Ombudsman, Women's Office, etc.).

The second element to be discussed in this section, the decision over controversial elections, in turn, has a more abundant literature available for consultation (Figueiredo, 2012; Magalhães, 1986; Porto, 2002; Ricci & Zulini, 2012). These works are concerned with understanding the specific role of the Election Certification Committee ('Comissão de Verificação de Poderes', a proprietary body of the BCD that adjudicated terms until 1930) in the politic dynamics, especially during the Republic.

Decisions over disputed elections in the form of the Election Certification Committee are partially based on the division of powers. Following a model that operates in many countries (Ricci & Zulini, 2012), it is an incumbency of the Legislative Branch itself to decide over the terms of its own members. Brazil adopted this practice from 1823 to 1930.

The first dispute process of an election occurred in 1823, still during the Constitutional Assembly before the establishment of the BCD (Porto, 2002). Through the course of the Empire, other solved disputes were reported, but the process for certifying elections gained notoriety during the Republic, especially in the administration of President Campos Sales (1898–1902). During that time, the politically unstable situation of the country, which was pressed by the noviceness of its Republic and also by the strength of federalism, was solved through a pact known as 'governor's politics' or 'state politics' (Lessa, 1988). In this pact, the federal government acknowledged and supported the state oligarchies and they supported the president of the Republic. The central mechanism of this process was the Election Certification Committee, which, from then on, assumed the power of 'filtering' local disputes, always with the intention to assure the permanence of the oligarchies that were installed in the states and the support of the federal government. During the Campos Sales administration, the president of the BCD in the previous legislature, or their vice-presidents, in the case of re-election, were to control the certifying process, which would establish political continuity and the exclusion of outsiders.

From 1889 to 1930 the literature (Magalhães, 1986, p. 76; Ricci & Zulini, 2013, p. 98) points to an average rate of exclusion/beheading of approximately 8.7 and 9.8 per cent, rising to 30 per cent as a maximum. This demonstrates the fragility of the electoral system and of representation and a strong oligarchical component in the acquisition and maintenance of political power and positions in the Legislative Branch. A paradox is created, for the BCD simultaneously defines the terms of its members, which constitutes power, and is also subject to the wider dynamics of Brazilian politics (the relationship between governors and president), which determines the composition of the

BCD and weakens it as an autonomous body. The BCD, in this situation, uses its own powers to subject itself to the executive officers.

Ricci and Zulini (2013), when facing international findings, conclude that the practice of certifying elections during the Old Republic was a factor favourable to the stability of the regime, and not for the instability. They also add that the exclusion procedure, in the Chamber of Deputies, was just the final step in a 'purification' process (p. 102) that initiated in the states in all the steps of the electoral process. Only the critical cases, when the opposition was sufficiently strong to win the local steps, were 'purified' in the Chamber. We should add that, most certainly, this stability of the regime is almost the opposite of democratic quality, since the political system was highly exclusive and the elections were frequently fraudulent. There was regime stability and weakening of the BCD through its subordination to the executive officers and a fictitious electoral representation.

This scenario was changed by the creation of a special court of justice (Electoral Justice) in the 1930s, to deal with the electoral procedures: organisation and inspection of the polls, and judgment of litigation. The idea of an electoral reform was present in the political movement that raised Vargas to power in 1930. As affirmed by Porto (2002, p. 258), in 1933 the legislative elections were already under the control of the Electoral Court and were a quiet event. This Court took the competence to decide over electoral results disputes away from the BCD and from all other legislative bodies of the country.

Thus, in terms of the institutionalisation of the BCD, what we see is a rupture process driven by external elements, not an internal process. A loss of competence happened; on the other hand, an increase of legitimacy and autonomy of its members and a strengthening of the electoral and representation link occurred.

Regarding the dynamics of the institutionalisation process, the advance of universal rules was not gradual, but the opposite. In the case of Brazil, the Legislative Branch lost its prerogative of validating the terms of its members due to a wider political process driven by the president of the Republic (the Executive Branch), which reconfigured the entire Brazilian electoral process. Thus, today, we have a mixed scenario: there are universal rules for entering the BCD, but the distribution of opportunities (specifically the positions in committees) depends on partisan agreements that refer, as a general rule, to other criteria excluding legislative experience or dedication to the legislative career.

Conclusions

The BCD has, at the same time, traits of institutional continuity and rupture. The continuity of its internal structures is notorious: the ruling bodies and their hierarchical relationship with the rest of the parliamentarians. With regards to ruptures, legislative careers were fractured many times by changes in the political regimen of the country. In the gaps between ruptures there is some continuity; however, the most recent findings in the literature seem to apply to the whole period: long-lived legislative careers are not the goal of Brazilian politicians. Another rupture that the BCD suffered was the one relating to the electoral system (which was changed from majoritarian to proportional in 1932) and the process of the adjudication rule of the terms. Regarding the last change, it was conducted by forces external to the parliament.

We can see that the process of institutionalisation happens in the wake of the dynamics of the wider political system. Until 1945, the electoral system and representation were fragile, and that limited the role of the BCD as a representative body. Just the same, its capacity for formulation, implementation and control of public policies has been historically small. Adding a multi-party system to that, the division of internal positions and opportunities through the proportional system and also the relative organisational complexity of the BCD, we can see that in the legislative-transformative-arena continuum, it cannot be placed in any of the extremes. The Chamber is not able to influence significantly the conduction of public policies and also does not exhibit to the public a clear vision of what the political forces in dispute are. This is a result of the sum of the internal characteristics of the BCD, the electoral system and the partisan system, and the historical weakness of representation in the country.

The basic issue regarding the institutionalisation of the BCD seems to be an insufficient development of democracy in Brazil. There is a representation gap, which is demonstrated by the short period with free, fair and involved elections. The democratic ruptures, even more so, have also robbed the parliament of its strength occasionally and of a possible prevalent position it might have had in the political scene.

The institutional development of the BCD has as its ingredients the influence of foreign institutional models (bicameralism, committees, etc.), when it falls in line with the Brazilian tradition of *bacharelismo* and of devotion to the models of advanced capitalist countries, but is especially linked to the Brazilian political tradition of patrimonialism, clientelism, high appreciation of state, etc. What we have today is a fairly large and costly legislative body that performs representation and governability activities at a mediocre level of effectivity. Democracy and BCD are evolving and will evolve together, and there is still a long way to go along the path of improvement.

Notes

1. The current annual budget of the BCD is R$5.27 billion (http://www.camara. leg.br/transparencia, accessed 10 May 2016), which, according to the exchange rate, which has been varying between R$3 and R$4, results in approximately US $1.5 billion.

2. The number of novice members is calculated in relation to the total number of deputies that have carried out terms, not in relation to the number of chairs, as established by the Polsby study (1968). Besides its importance to the establishment of the actual number of novices in the House, this decision can be justified by the fact that there is not, especially for the older periods, a precise control of resignations, leaves, substitutions, etc.

3. There is a literature already established about career patterns in the BCD, but it deals especially with the post-1945 period. Cf. Santos (1999), which discusses aspects of the institutionalisation according to Polsby (1968) and also Samuels (2003), Perissinotto (2013), Marenco and Serna (2007) and Matos (2011).

4. A senator of the Empire, Nabuco de Araújo, thus defined the Brazilian electoral system in his time: 'the Moderating Branch [the Emperor] is able to invoke whoever it wants to organize Ministries: this person executes the election, because it has to; this election makes the majority. This is the representative system of our country' (quoted in Chacon, 2007, p. 11).

5. During the Empire the political dynamics involved succession between the conservative and liberal sectors, and the year of 1860 saw a renewal of liberal offices, after almost 14 years of a conservative majority.

6. The analysis happened through the identification of terms that nominate the bodies of the BCD, with exclusive attention to the existence or non-existence of certain words, as claimed by infometrical studies (Robredo & Cunha, 1998). Thus, there is no evaluation of activities and competencies in seeking similarities or patterns.

7. We should also consider that the positions in the Directive Board and the presidencies of the commissions follow the principle of partisan proportionality, and are distributed among all of the parties according to their number of deputies.

8. See, in this issue, an article by J. de Souza Pinto.

Disclosure statement

No potential conflict of interest was reported by the authors.

References

Aguiar, O. O. (2015). *As Regras Informais e o Processo Decisório na Câmara dos Deputados* [Informal rules and the decision process in Brazilian Chamber of Deputies] (Master's thesis). Brasília: Cefor, Câmara dos Deputados.

Benevides, M. V. (1981). *A UDN e o udenismo* [The UDN and the "udenismo"]. Rio de Janeiro: Paz e Terra.

Benevides, M. V. (1989). *O PTB e o trabalhismo: partido e sindicato em São Paulo: 1945-1964* [PTB and "trabalhismo": Party and union in São Paulo: 1945-1964]. São Paulo: Brasiliense.

Braga, R. J. (2014). A agenda legislativa do governo Castelo Branco: um regime político em transição [The legislative agenda of the government Castelo Branco: A political regime in transition]. *E-Legis*, 7(14), 87–105. Retrieved from http://e-legis.camara.leg.br/cefor/index.php/e-legis/article/view/194

Brasil. (1826, May 17). *Regimento Interno da Câmara dos Deputados* [Bylaws of Brazilian Chamber of Deputies]. Rio de Janeiro: Typographia Nacional.

Brasil. (1832/1931, September 3). *Regimento Interno da Câmara dos Deputados* [Bylaws of Brazilian Chamber of Deputies]. Rio de Janeiro: Typographia Nacional.

Brasil. (1874). *Regimento Interno da Câmara dos Deputados* [Bylaws of Brazilian Chamber of Deputies]. Changes in January 20th, 1874. Rio de Janeiro: Typographia Nacional.

Brasil. (1899). *Regimento Interno da Câmara dos Deputados: nova edição com alterações aprovadas pela Câmara dos Srs. Deputados)* [Bylaws of Brazilian Chamber of Deputies: New edition]. Rio de Janeiro: Imprensa Nacional.

Brasil. (1904, December 28). *Regimento Interno da Câmara dos Deputados* [Bylaws of Brazilian Chamber of Deputies]. Rio de Janeiro: Diário do Congresso Nacional. p. 3876/87.

Brasil. (1915). *Regimento Interno da Câmara dos Deputados: consolidação de todas as disposições aprovadas* [Bylaws of Brazilian Chamber of Deputies: Approved changes]. Rio de Janeiro: Imprensa Nacional.

Brasil. (1921). *Regimento Interno da Câmara dos Deputados: com indices systematicos* [Bylaws of Brazilian Chamber of Deputies: With systematic indexes]. Rio de Janeiro: Imprensa Nacional.

Brasil. (1928). *Regimento Interno e Constituição da República* [Bylaws of Brazilian Chamber of Deputies and Brazil's Constitution]. Rio de Janeiro: Imprensa Nacional.

Brasil. (1946). *Assembléia Constituinte* [Constituent Assembly]. Resolução n.1, de 12 de março de 1946. *Regimento Interno.* Rio de Janeiro: Diário do Poder Legislativo.

Brasil. (1949). *Resolução da Câmara dos Deputados n. 34 de 1949: Promulga o Regimento Interno da Câmara dos Deputados* [Brazilian Chamber of Deputies' resolution: Promulgates the Bylaws of Brazilian Chamber of Deputies]. Rio de Janeiro: Diário do Congresso Nacional. 20/08/1949, p. 7377.

Brasil. (1972). *Resolução da Câmara dos Deputados n. 30 de 1972. Dispõe sobre o Regimento interno* [Brazilian Chamber of Deputies' resolution: Bylaws of Brazilian Chamber of Deputies]. Section 1. Suplement A. 01/11/1972. Brasília: Diário do Congresso Nacional. p. 1.

Brasil. (1989/2011). *Regimento interno da Câmara dos Deputados* [Bylaws of Brazilian Chamber of Deputies] (9th ed.). Série textos básicos ; n. 63. Brasília: Câmara dos Deputados, Edições Câmara, 179 p.

Brasil. (2014). *Regimento Interno da Câmara dos Deputados* [Bylaws of Brazilian Chamber of Deputies] (13th ed.). Série textos básicos, n. 81. Brasília: Câmara dos Deputados, Edições Câmara.

Carvalho, J. M. (1996). *A Construção da ordem: a elite politica imperial; teatro de sombras: a politica imperial* [Construction of the order: The imperial political elite; shadow theater: The imperial policy]. Rio de Janeiro: Ufrj Relume Dumara Press.

Chacon, V. (2007). *História do legislativo brasileiro* [History of the Brazilian legislature] (Vol. 3). Brasília: Senado Federal, Subsecretaria Especial do Interlegis.

Dahl, R.A. (1997). *Poliarquia: participação e oposição* [Polyarchy: Participation and opposition]. (Classicos: 9). São Paulo: Edusp Press.

Faoro, R. (2009). *Os donos do poder: formação do patronato político brasileiro* [Power owners: Formation of the Brazilian political patronage]. São Paulo: Globo.

Figueiredo, A., & Limongi, F. (2001). *Executivo e Legislativo na Nova Ordem Constitucional* [Executive and legislative branches in New Constitutional Order] (2nd ed.). Rio de Janeiro: FGV.

Figueiredo, V. F. (2012). *O papel da Comissão Verificadora de Poderes da Câmara Federal para a articulação do Estado Brasileiro durante a Primeira República* [The role of the testing Commission powers of the Brazilian Chamber of Deputies for the coordination of the Brazilian State during the First Republic]. Paper presented at the meeting of the XVIII Encontro Regional of ANPUH, Mariana.

Fleischer, D. (2007). Os partidos políticos. In L. Avelar & A. O. Cintra (Eds.), *Sistema político brasileiro: uma introdução* [Brazilian Political System: An introduction]. (2nd ed., pp. 303–348). Rio de Janeiro: Konrad-Adenauer-Stiftung. São Paulo: Unesp Press.

Guimarães, A. S., Schwartz, F. P., Souza, J. W., & Melo, M. R. M. (2015). Strategic management in legislative public management: A comparative perspective. *International Business and Management, 11*, 13–24.

Hibbing, J. R. (1988). Legislative institutionalization with illustrations from the British House of Commons. *American Journal of Political Science, 32*(3), 681–712.

Hippolito, L. (1985). *De raposas e reformistas: o PSD e a experiência democrática brasileira, 1945–64* [Foxes and reformers: The PSD and the Brazilian democratic experience, 1945–64]. Rio de Janeiro: Paz e Terra.

Lessa, R. A. (1988). *Invenção Republicana: Campos Sales, as bases e a decadência da Primeira República* [The Invention Republican: Campos Sales, the bases and the decay of the First Republic]. São Paulo: Vértice.

Llanos, M., & Nolte, D. (2003). Bicameralism in the Americas: Around the extremes of symmetry and incongruence. *Journal of Legislative Studies, 9*(3), autumn, 54–86.

Magalhães, M.C.C. (1986). *O mecanismo das comissões verificadoras de poderes: estabilidade e dominação política (1894–1930)* [The mechanism of verifiers commission powers: Stability and political domination (1894–1930)] (Doctoral Thesis). Universidade de Brasília, Brasília.

Marenco, A. (2007). Devagar se vai ao longe? In C. R. MELO & M. ALCÁNTARA SÁEZ (Eds.), *A Democracia Brasileira: Balanço e perspectivas para o século 21* [Brazilian democracy: Current situation and prospects for the 21st century] (pp. 73–105). Belo Horizonte: UFMG Press.

Marenco, A., & Serna, M. (2007). Por Que Carreiras Políticas na Esquerda e na Direita Não São Iguais? Recrutamento Legislativo em Brasil, Chile e Uruguai [Why careers policies on the left and right are not equal? Legislative recruitment in Brazil, Chile and Uruguay]. *RBCS, 22*(64), 93–113.

Massicotte, L. (2001). Legislative unicameralism: A global survey and a few case studies. [s.l.] *The Journal of Legislative Studies, 7*, 151–170.

Matos, V. L. C. (2011). O impacto das eleições municipais na representação da Câmara dos Deputados: Deputados Federais Candidatos a Prefeito. In J. Nicolau & R. J. Braga (Eds.), *Para além das urnas: reflexões sobre a Câmara dos Deputados* [Beyond the voting polls: Reflections about Brazilian Chamber of Deputies] (pp. 65–89). Brasília: Edições Câmara.

Miranda, R. C. R. (2012). Gestão do conhecimento estratégico na Câmara dos Deputados: uma avaliação teórico-sistêmica. In R. C. R. Miranda (Ed.), *Informação e Conhecimento no Legislativo* [Information and Knowledge in the Legislature] (1 ed., Vol. 1, pp. 141–162). Brasília: Edições Câmara.

Nunes, E. O. (2010). *A gramática política do Brasil: clientelismo, corporativismo e insulamento burocrático* [The political grammar of Brazil: Clientelism, corporatism and bureaucratic insulation]. Rio de Janeiro: Garamond.

Opello, Jr., W. C. (1986). Portugal's parliament: An organizational analysis of legislative performance. *Legislative Studies Quarterly, 11*(3), 291–319.

Perissinotto, R. M. (2013). As transformações da classe política brasileira nos séculos XIX, XX e XXI: um estudo do perfil sócio-político dos deputados federais (1889–2014) [The changes in the Brazilian political class in the nineteenth, twentieth and twenty-first centuries: A study of the socio-political profile of members of Congress (1889–2014]. Unpublished research sumited to MCTI/CNPq/MEC/CAPES. n. 43.

Pires, J. M. (2011). A implantação da representação proporcional de lista aberta no Brasil. In J. Nicolau & R. J. Braga (Eds.), *Para além das urnas: reflexões sobre a Câmara dos Deputados* [Beyond the voting polls: Reflections about Brazilian Chamber of Deputies] (pp. 21–44). Brasília: Edições Câmara.

Polsby, N. W. (1968). The institutionalization of the U.S. House of Representatives. *American Political Science Review, 62*(1), p. 144–168.

Polsby, N. W. (1975). Legislatures. In F. I. Greenstein & N. Polsby (Orgs.), *Handbook of political science*. Boston: Addison-Wesley. Retrieved from http://works.bepress.com/nelson_polsby/18/

Porto, W. C. (2002). *O voto* no Brasil: da colônia à 6ª República [The vote in Brazil: From colony era to the 6th Republic]. (2nd ed.). Rio de Janeiro: Topbooks.

Ricci, P., & Zulini, J. P. (2012). 'Beheading', rule manipulation and fraud: The approval of election results in Brazil, 1894–1930. *Journal of Latin American Studies*, 44(03), 495–521. doi:10.1017/S0022216X12000764

Ricci, P., & Zulini, J. P. (2013). Quem Ganhou as Eleições? A Validação dos Resultados antes da Criação da Justiça Eleitoral [Who won the electionValidation of the results before the creation of the Electoral Justice]. *Revista de Sociologia E Política*, Curitiba, 21(45), 91–105.

Robredo, J., & Cunha, M. B. (1998). Aplicação de técnicas infométricas para identificar a abrangência do léxico básico que caracteriza os processos de indexação e recuperação da informação [Infometric thecniques appplicated to identify the scope of the basic lexicon that features the process of information Indexing and Retrieval]. *Ci. Inf., Brasília*, 27(1), 11–27. Retrieved from www.scielo.br/scielo.php?script=sci_arttext&pid=S0100-19651998000100003&lng=en&nrm=iso

Rogers, J. R. (2003). The impact of bicameralism on legislative production. [s.l.] *Legislative Studies Quarterly*, 28, 509–528.

Samuels, D. (2003). *Ambition, federalism, and legislative politics in Brazil*. New York, NY: Cambridge University Press.

Santos, F. (1999). Recruitment and retention of legislators in brazil. *Legislative Studies Quaterly*, 24(2), 209–237.

Shell, D. (2001). The history of bicameralism. [s.l.] *The Journal of Legislative Studies*, 7, 5–18.

Souza, M. C. C. (1990). *Estado e Partidos Políticos no Brasil: 1930–1964* (3rd ed.). [State and Political Parties in Brazil: 1930–1964]. São Paulo: Alfa-Ômega.

Vatter, A. (2005). Bicameralism and policy performance: The effects of cameral structure in comparative perspective. [s.l.] *The Journal of Legislative Studies*, 11, 194–215.

The legislative and public policies in Brazil: before and after the 1988 Constitution

Julio Roberto de Souza Pinto

ABSTRACT
This paper examines the Legislative's role in defining public policies in Brazil before and after the 1988 Constitution. It shows that the main social rights were institutionalised during the dictatorships of Getúlio Vargas (1930–34, 1937–45) and the military (1964–85), periods during which Congress was either closed or worked only decoratively. Although strengthened by the 1988 Constitution, Congress continues to play a secondary role in relation to the president, a position that in recent years it has been forced to share with the Supreme Court. Finally, it indicates that Congress, thus emptied of power, has turned its energies to expand its own privileges, causing popular outrage. It concludes that it is precisely by taking the opposite direction, turning to society, expanding representation to include women, afro-descendants, natives and other social minorities, and making itself more permeable to popular participation and control, that Congress may qualify itself as the main institutional space of political decision-making in Brazil.

Introduction

Throughout the history of Brazilian politics, public policies[1] have been basically defined by the Executive, with little or, at least in some periods, no legislative involvement. The political agreement that brought the country back to democracy, whose main expression was the 1988 Constitution, gave more importance to Congress in the public policy-making process. The president, however, remained as the leading actor.

In recent years, Congress has had to share its secondary role in defining public policies with another actor who has been gaining prominence: the Supreme Court. The Supreme Court's growing role in the public policy-making process has been reinforced by the equally growing process of rationalisation in modern societies, a phenomenon that in Brazil has been observed and discussed since the military's attempt to deploy an 'efficient democracy' and, after the sequence of social democrat governments initiated by Fernando Henrique Cardoso in 1995, has gained new strength in the current, interim government of Michel Temer. Both the military and the current interim government seem to find a certain incompatibility between democracy and efficiency, leaning to favour the latter over the former.

Limited in their role of defining public policies, both houses of Congress, the Chamber of Deputies and the Senate, have channelled all their efforts to expand the already vast privileges of their members, which, among other factors, has since June 2013 led millions of Brazilians to the streets across the country to protest against Congress's lack of representativeness.

After examining the Legislative's skimpy role in defining public policies in Brazil both before and after the 1988 Constitution, this paper concludes by pointing to the opening to society – through expanding representation to include women, afro-descendants, natives and other social minorities, and through expanding transparency and permeability to create more effective mechanisms for popular participation and control – as a possible path to Congress's qualification as the main institutional forum for discussing and defining public policies in Brazil.

Defining public policy in Brazil before the 1988 Constitution

Since the creation of the Brazilian state in 1822 – formalised in the 1824 Constitution – up to the institution of the regime enshrined in the 1988 Constitution, the Legislative had exercised, most of the time, a secondary role in relation to the Executive in the public policy-making process.

Brazil became independent from Portugal on 7 September 1822 through a joint action of liberals and conservatives. Yet, over them was hovering Portuguese Prince Dom Pedro, acclaimed and crowned as the Emperor of Brazil on 1 December, invested with an authority that pre-existed the first Brazilian Constitution. Dom Pedro I made this very clear in his speech opening the Constituent Assembly, when he promised to obey the Constitution 'if it were worthy of Brazil and of himself' (Faoro, 2012). Later on, as he realised that this condition, as far as he was concerned, would not be sustained, he dissolved the Constituent Assembly and instituted a constitution of his own.

Under the 1824 Constitution, the Emperor, as the Moderating Power, would have the role of arbitrating political disputes. In reality, however, the Crown, invested with the power freely to appoint and dismiss ministers, kept command of both politics and administration, converting the first Brazilian government system into just a semblance of parliamentarism.

Among the three political bodies set up to mitigate the supremacy of the Emperor, two (the State Council[2] and the Senate) were appointed for life by the Crown and the other (the Chamber of Deputies) was elected to a temporary mandate. The elections, nevertheless, were inauthentic, not so much due to the census suffrage, which restricted the number of voters, but due to social circumstances, which selected the deliberative body, and legal circumstances, which filtered the voters' will. Only between 1 and 3 per cent of the population participated in the formation of the 'national will', a rate that would not change substantially in the first 40 years of the Republic (Faoro, 2012). Reduced in its importance, weight and density, it is no wonder that the lifetime Senate controlled the temporary Chamber, which in turn was controlled by an aristocratic bureaucracy that surrounded Dom Pedro I and, later on, his son and successor, Dom Pedro II.

Switching from a unitary to a federal state and from a monarchic to a republican government on 15 November 1889 did not change significantly the situation. Power would no longer be the expression of the centre, of the alliance between the hereditary throne and lifetime categories, on the one hand, and the wealth and credit holders with strong ties to the international financial system, on the other. It would irradiate from territorial camps, grouped regionally in the provinces. However, despite the liberal rhetoric, the shift was not a result of the people's action, but of social strata that were enabled by wealth and credit, both national and international, to speak on its behalf, in scattered tutelage that came to replace the imperial, concentrated one.

The military proclaimed and initially conducted the Federal Republic.

For now, the government's colour is purely military. The fact was theirs, theirs alone, because the collaboration of the civil element was almost nil. The people saw that bestialized, astonished, surprised, not knowing what it meant. Many believed sincerely to be watching a military parade

wrote Aristides Lobo, one of the signatories of the Republic Proclamation (Faoro, 2012, p. 555).

Bit by bit, the new regime showed its liberal but not democratic face, differing little from the previous one. A 'politics of governors', grounded in an election enticement by the 'colonels', would provide stability to the system. Covering much more than ordaining it normatively, the 1891 Constitution would give legitimacy to a social and political structure that resisted major changes. The same imperial practice would continue to operate, in which the constitutional fictions assumed the character of a disguise, so that, under the shadow of an artificially assembled legitimacy, social and political forces imposed themselves without obedience to printed forms. It was the old constitutional hypocrisy, so harshly denounced by critics of the ancient regime, which would persist throughout the following decades.

The transition in the command was done gradually. The imperial system began from the centre, and expanded over the appointed and not elected presidents of the provinces, using an instrument manipulated vertically from the court, the National Guard. In the Republic's early years, while the military headed government and the now-called governors kept being appointed, the structure had not undergone substantial change. Nevertheless, as the governors started being elected, the decision-axis shifted to the now-called states, leaving larger states increasingly unscathed from interference from the centre, the latter ensuring and strengthening itself through the allurement of smaller states, a movement that culminates in the 'governors' politics'. It is in this context that the 'colonels' stood out in alliance with the state oligarchies. The colonel got his name from the National Guard, whose head of the municipal garrison received that denomination. Beside the legally appointed colonel, there was also the traditional colonel, who was also a political leader and master of the means capable of sustaining the lifestyle of his position. The colonel, nevertheless, did not command because he had wealth; rather, he commanded because he had this power recognised in an unwritten pact. It was a non-rational, pre-bureaucratic, traditional type of power. Let no one imagine that between the colonel and the simple voter reigned brutality. The colonel was, above all, a comrade. The voter voted for the candidate indicated by the colonel not because he was afraid of the pressure, but because of a sacred duty, that tradition forged (Faoro, 2012).

In the Republic, as well as in the Monarchy, elections were a mere legitimating instrument of economic and political forces, not an expression of the 'national will', as trumpeted by the liberals. This, of course, kept Congress and their houses as regional oligarchies' hostages. Congress's 'Credentials Verification Committee', then in charge of overseeing the Brazilian electoral system, did not ratify elected lawmakers who did not support the 'governors' policy'.

On 5 July 1922, the shootings at the Copacabana Fort heralded the end of the 'Old Republic'. It was necessary to free the countryside from the colonel, and the states from the oligarchies, in an anti-traditional movement. An interventionist state would crown the project, to be carried out by the only category able to structure and sustain it, the Army. The anti-oligarchic movement, however, had not met by then the necessary and sufficient conditions to thrive.

It was eight years later when political leaders of the states of Minas Gerais, Rio Grande do Sul and Paraíba, rebelling against São Paulo's hegemony and joining what remained of the 1922 movement, put an end to the Old Republic and brought Getúlio Vargas to power. Yet, even though in their discourse the men who took power on 3 November 1930 were adverse to the 'governors' politics', they would behave within its boundaries. As soon as the revolution was crowned victorious and some political reforms were undertaken, with the introduction of the secret ballot and judicial oversight of the electoral process, São Paulo would return to lead the 'renewed Republic'.

By imposition of São Paulo, Vargas was bound to convene a new Constituent Assembly, which would produce the 1934 Constitution. The new Constitution, though, would not curb the floodgates opened in 1930 for much longer. In the government's leadership, there was not a constitutional president, but a popular myth, a driver of an ongoing revolution. The reforms, aimed at protecting the proletariat and accommodating the expanding middle class, beside those that would lead to economic development and to the country's emancipation, would not be possible within the framework outlined by a Constituent Assembly dominated by liberals and conservatives.

It was under Vargas's dictatorial regime (1930–34, 1937–45), during which Congress was kept closed, that the most important social policies were implemented in Brazil. In the labour area, there was: the regulation of the working day, set at eight hours; women's work with the prohibition of night work and lower salaries for women; minors' work; paid annual leave and minimum wage; and labour rights later consolidated in the Consolidation of Labour Laws (CLT) 1943, until today the primary legal statute governing labour relations in Brazil (Carvalho, 2013; Santos, 1987). In the social security area, the Institute of Retirement and Pension for Maritime was created, initiating a process of transformation and strengthening of the retirement and pension funds instituted in the previous decade (Carvalho, 2013).

The export model of tropical products and raw materials and of manufactured goods import characterised Brazil's economy in the first three decades of the twentieth century. This pattern had already begun to be questioned in the second half of the previous century. Nevertheless, it was with the World War of 1914–18 and the coffee crisis that it underwent the most drastic fluctuations. The 1930 Revolution symbolised the break with that model. The manufactured goods import substitution model developed rapidly from 1930 to 1962 (Ianni, 1988). The succession of political crises in this period indicates the growing conflict between the developmental and independent nationalism, on one side, and the preservation of ties and commitments to traditional society and the international economic system controlled by North Atlantic powers, on the other.

In the period 1946–64, Brazil not only enjoyed strong economic growth and its most significant and lasting reduction in inequality (Souza & Medeiros, 2015), but also had its first democratic experience. Additionally, Brazil reached one of its most intense, dynamic and meaningful moments as far as the class struggle was concerned. Notwithstanding, both liberals and conservatives have attributed to this period – especially to the João Goulart government (1961–64) – only negative aspects: 'political turmoil', 'crisis of authority' and 'administrative chaos'; runaway inflation and economic recession; breakdown of hierarchy and discipline in the military; and 'subversion' of law and order, and advancement of left and communising forces, among other ills (Toledo, 2004).

Throughout Brazilian republican history, the blow to the country's fragile political institutions has been a permanent threat. Its ghost had haunted particularly the democratic governments post-1946, with greater intensity from the 1960s onwards. The Goulart government was born, lived and died under the *coup d'état* spectrum. On 1 April 1964, the coup, persistently claimed by sectors of civil society, would then be fully victorious. At this point, it is worth noting that all *coups d'état* that occurred in Brazil were widely and blatantly supported by the military. One can even say that it has been the normal way of succession in power in societies where the oligarchies and mass policies prevail over political parties, a phenomenon that in itself reveals the failure of the liberal model adopted by dependent and semi-dependent countries such as Brazil.

The 1964 coup, among other things, sought to stop the democratic claims expressed in the demand for expanding urban and rural workers' citizenship. Although prohibited by the then rigid labour legislation, the General Workers' Command (CGT) had an outstanding performance in the Brazilian political scene. Together with other lower ranking unions, the CGT was responsible for the first explicitly political strikes in Brazilian history. To the disgust of the rightist sectors, the president received CGT leaders in the palace and important party leaders recognised them as interlocutors. The conservative press designated the CGT as the 'fourth power', reinforcing the myth, forged at the time of Vargas, according to which Goulart aimed to establish a 'syndicalist Republic' in the country.

The populist character of the Goulart government was manifested clearly and exemplarily here. The actions of the unions – through their strikes in defence of either economic or political demands – were tolerated and even encouraged by Goulart, as they served the national development project. However, the political control of the CGT by independent trade union leaders – for example, by the Brazilian Communist Party[3] and the 'compact group' of the Brazilian Labour Party – had always been fought by Goulart and his union advisors. Throughout the period, Goulart had showed clear preference for leaders and trade union organisations that, in exchange for their political and ideological independence, were ready to receive government's favours and benefits.

The 1964 coup, therefore, came to crown the previously failed attempts. After all, re-establishing the accumulation process would require a prior disarticulation of defence and pressure instruments of the popular classes. To contain the 'pressure from below', measures should be taken to extinguish not only the populist regime, but also the bourgeoisie's very direct political expression.

In fact, the military and a sector of the bourgeoisie made an agreement. The latter gave up part of the traditional political controls (party system, elections, etc.) and tools of symbol definition and ideological diffusion (press freedom, habeas corpus, doctrinal pluralism, liberal education), as well as economic regulation. In return, the military assumed implicitly the business owners' economic interests as if they were those of the nation, and reserved some areas for their economic activities.

The coup of 1964, therefore, displaced the national-bourgeois sector and the developmental statist group from the hegemonic position they had been keeping, in favour of a more internationalised sector of the bourgeoisie. The economy was then integrated more widely and deeply into the capitalist world-system.

Of course, this change in the economic development pattern and in the correlation of forces that sustained it had taken place before 1964. From Juscelino Kubitschek's government (1956–61) onwards, the development model that was born in the late 1930s, gained strength during the war and became a relatively clear policy during Vargas's second government (1950–54), started winding down. State, national capital and foreign investment had been the spring for development. With Kubitschek's economic policy of rapid industrialisation and expansion of industrial mass consumption (urban middle class), the social and political bases of the populist regime (whether in its authoritarian or democratic stage) began failing to match the sectors that controlled the productive forces.

Moreover, the capitalist world-economy had also undergone major changes in the previous decade. International corporations had come to diversify not only the branches of economic activity under their control, but also the location of plants, moving some of them to peripheral areas. This led to greater interdependence in the international productive sphere – when the capitalist world-economy was seen from the angle of decision centres – and a change in the forms of dependence that affected the peripheral countries. In this new context, social groups expressing international capitalism – whether composed of Brazilians, foreigners, or both – gained importance. Other sectors gaining influence were the military and bureaucracy, which, being unpopular, had been excluded in the previous system (Cardoso, 1993).

Interestingly, despite the so-called 'economic miracle' often associated with this period, the long decline in inequality observed until the early 1960s was followed by a big jump in 1964, the year of the coup. From then onwards, the richest 1 per cent share of income had grown a lot in a short period of time, reversing the previous trend. In the early 1970s, it had already reached the same levels of the 1950s (Souza & Medeiros, 2015).

Even though the 1964 coup sought, among other things, to suppress the increasing demand for social inclusion and deliberately fostered a re-concentration of income, resulting in a sudden interruption in the long decline of inequality verified in the previous two decades, paradoxically, it was during the military dictatorship that the social security system was unified through the creation, in 1966, of the National Institute for Social Security, and categories so far kept out of the system were finally included. Rural workers were incorporated in 1971 through the establishment of the Rural Assistance Fund. Domestic workers and the self-employed were included in 1972 and 1973, respectively (Carvalho, 2013). These facts corroborate the argument put forth in this paper according to which the main social policies in force in Brazil were set during dictatorial periods when Congress was closed or worked only decoratively.

Politically, the 1964 coup led to another paradox. On the one hand, it was a typical military regime as the armed forces ran the country. Such a situation would make the military institution become an arena of struggle for political power. Conflicts between moderate and radical officials permeated the 25 years[4] of military influence, generating frequent political instability. On the other hand, the military kept the mechanisms and procedures of representative democracy at work: the legislative and the judiciary were operational, despite having their powers harshly reduced and several of their members purged; alternation in the presidency of the Republic was maintained; periodic elections were held, albeit under controls of various kinds; and political parties were kept running, even though under drastic restrictions (Kinzo, 2001).

Indeed, the military carried out a 'sanitisation' of politics in Brazil through marginalising the national leaders and fragmentising the party structure, which resulted in a political and administrative vacuum that came to be filled by techno-entrepreneurs and the military. Politicians became ancillary. Reforms in policy-making channels excluded traditional politicians and, at the same pace, favoured the participation of the technocrats (Dreifuss & Dulci, 2008). Behind all this lay a preference for economism or development-alism at the expense of freedom. The justifying argument for this predilection was twofold: on one side, the discipline required for economic development (wage restraint policies, income concentration mechanisms, effectiveness in the implementation of decisions, 'militarisation' of society to achieve high growth rates of the national product, etc.); on the other side, the 'enemy' (unionists, socialists and progressives in general), who in a climate of freedom would prevent or hinder the efforts towards 'nation building' (Cardoso, 1993).

It was not just the military regime that was peculiar in Brazil. The re-democ-ratisation process also revealed peculiarities. It might have been the longest case of democratic transition in the world: a slow and gradual liberalising process, which took 11 years for civilians to resume power and a further five years for the president to be elected by popular vote. The rise of General Ernesto Geisel to power in 1974 and the announcement of his project of 'slow, gradual and safe' transition marked the beginning of the democratisation process. The way this liberalisation project was conducted and the dynamics of the political process that eventually led to democracy were largely driven by the military or, more precisely, by one of their political and ideological currents.

Such a re-democratisation process corresponded more to the need for the military to resolve problems internal to their corporation than to a sudden democratic conversion by the officer corps. The control that the military had on the state and its ostensive presence on the political scene ended up bringing a series of political and ideological conflicts within the military apparatus, subverting the traditional hierarchy and the command chains. The transformation of the 'political model' was not originally conceived as the military's return to barracks, but as the expulsion of politics from within them (Codato, 2005).

The original design of the dictatorial regime's liberalisation was not identical to the political process that it unleashed, though. Once started, the movement acquired its own logic. The various crises in the last two military governments had to do with attempts by both presidents to reassert their control over the process and the civil and military opposition to change it. The dynamics that the process took cannot be explained solely by ideological or personal disputes within the military apparatus. The passage from the industrial capital hegemony to the financial capital hegemony illustrates the redefinition of relations between classes and the military, attested by the protests of workers and middle-class professionals.

By 1982, the opposition party, the Party of the Brazilian Democratic Movement (PMDB), already controlled around 50 per cent of the electorate, while the ruling party controlled only 36 per cent (Codato, 2005). Parallel to the evolution of opposition parties, the last two military governments had to face a more modern form of political organisation, the 'new unionism'. It consisted of a different way of organising workers in comparison with the union linked to the state, created after 1930, and a different way of presenting wage demands. The key point was the attempt to negotiate directly with companies, without the mediation of the Ministry of Labour. The jump from 118 shutdowns in 1978 to 2193 in 1987 must have had some influence on the regime change process (Codato, 2005).

Perhaps it is accurate to say that the political opening was the result of two dynamics that acted simultaneously in the political system: the dynamics of negotiation within the realm of the elites and the dynamics of societal pressures on the state. The former established the content, defined the mode and imposed the nature of the transition; the latter determined its pace.

In 1984, the PMDB proposed a constitutional amendment to restore the direct vote for president. In order to get popular support for the adoption of the amendment, the PMDB and other opposition parties – among which was the newly created Workers' Party (PT) – mobilised millions of people at rallies throughout Brazil. Although the 'Direct Elections Now' campaign was the most popular event thus far registered in the country, the amendment was defeated in a Congress still controlled by the military.

For the opposition forces, there were two choices left: either seeking dissident sympathisers within the government or breaking the rules by mobilising civil society. The PMDB, specifically its moderate wing, which was the most numerous and led the party, was in favour of the first option. In favour of the second alternative was the PT, followed by a small group of PMDB lawmakers who maintained close relations with social movements.

In fact, while the PMDB worked for the 'Direct Elections Now' campaign, the party's moderate wing was already articulating an alternative strategy should the amendment not pass in Congress: Tancredo Neves would run as the opposition candidate in the indirect election for president. However, to achieve this, it was necessary to get support from the other side of the aisle, i.e. from ruling party lawmakers. The opportunity arose when some ruling party lawmakers refused to support the government-appointed candidate. In exchange for dissidents' support of the candidacy of Neves, Senator José Sarney was chosen to be the candidate for vice-president on the opposition ticket. Neves won the indirect elections, but never took office. With his sudden death, Sarney was sworn in as the first civilian president since the 1964 coup.

In short, during the monarchic period, the Legislative was weak and controlled by the Emperor and the aristocratic bureaucracy that surrounded him; so it was, with minor variations, throughout the republican period until the 1988 Constitution. During the Old Republic, Congress continued to be elected through the same fraudulent process. The novelty was that by this time the oligarchies that controlled it were decentralised regionally under the state of São Paulo hegemony.

During the Vargas dictatorship, Congress was kept closed. With the removal of Vargas but under the new electoral rules established by him, a new legislature was elected, and Brazil had its first democratic experience. Congress, however, remained dominated by conservative forces. In fact, despite having resorted to mass politics, the 1930 Revolution did so to allow intra-elite power exchange between a group fully integrated to the international commodities market and another whose interests were focused on national industry development. No wonder Congress offered strong opposition to the policies of wealth redistribution and social inclusion begun by Vargas and carried forward by the following democratic governments.

The 1964 military coup reversed this situation, proving to be a counter-revolution, though it included in the social security system categories hitherto left out, thus completing the work initialised during the Vargas dictatorship. All this supports the argument put forward in this paper according to which, throughout the period that preceded the 1988 Constitution, the Legislative had little or, at times, no participation in the process of defining public policies in Brazil. It has been shown in the narrative of Brazilian political history thus far constructed that the most important social rights were recognised and guaranteed during dictatorships, periods when Congress was closed or worked only perfunctorily.

Defining public policy in Brazil before the 1988 Constitution

The so-called 'New Republic' (1985–89), the last government of the military dictatorship cycle, put an end to the long democratic transition by establishing political hegemony of the opposition to the regime (1986), promulgating a constitution (1988) and conducting a popular election for president (1989). One outcome of this long and controlled political transition, nevertheless, was the continued authoritarianism and the continuing predominance of the Executive over the Legislative. After all, the victory of Geisel and the military that led the liberalisation process against the so-called 'hard line' was obtained by an increase of authoritarianism, not the other way around. The longevity of the party that supported the military and parties that originated from it indicates that there has been no real replacement of the groups in power, but rather a reaccommodation within the elites.

José Sarney's government (1985–90) was the ultimate expression of the iron circle that had successfully managed political change in Brazil. The slogan of the alliance that, with Tancredo Neves's death, took Sarney to power – 'conciliation' and 'social pact' – succeeded in neutralising both the attempts to oppose the dictatorial regime that emerged in the 1977–80 conjuncture (strikes, grass-roots social movements, and corporative protests against 'state intervention in the economy') and the Direct Elections Now campaign in 1984. The result was the improvement of an anti-populist and anti-popular regime or a neither explicitly dictatorial nor fully democratic political form. It was the last government, civil, of a series of authoritarian governments in Brazil. There was no actual break with authoritarianism but a transformation – slow, gradual and safe.

Despite all this, Brazil's re-democratisation process ran its course. Regarding social and economic issues, the path was tortuous in the following period: between 1986 and 1994, the country changed its currency four times and had six experiments in economic stabilisation, only the last – the Real Plan – having been successful. The succession of failures not only aggravated the economic and social crisis, but also compromised governability.

The drafting of the 1988 Constitution was illustrative of the complexity that surrounded the democratisation process in Brazil. From start to finish, the process had involved a clash between various groups, each trying to increase or restrict the boundaries of social, economic and political arrangements to be established. Indeed, this atmosphere of verbal battle and backstage manoeuvres was largely a side effect of the transition course. A refounding grounded in a negotiated settlement was pressed in two directions: in one direction, by the political forces of the ancient regime trying to secure their place in the new scenario; and in the other direction, by leftist sectors that, although a minority, had acquired an important role in the constitutional process.

The taint of being a negotiated transition made its drivers – moderate political leaders – become more vulnerable to critiques about the limitations of the new regime and therefore more sensitive to pressure by political forces that called for the deepening of the democratisation process. Because of this factor, it is likely that the constitutional structure has become much more democratic than would be expected in the circumstances of a transition process as gradual and controlled as was the Brazilian. Thus, despite having been widely critiqued at the time for its parliamentary nature, the 1987–88 Constituent Assembly certainly was the most democratic experience in Brazilian constitutional history.

With regard to its product, in spite of various imperfections, the 1988 Constitution represented a significant advance. All the mechanisms of representative democracy have been secured, even those associated with direct democracy, such as the referendum and the right of popular legislative initiative. In addition, power has been decentralised as a result of the strengthening the legislative, the judiciary and subnational levels of government, as well as total freedom to organise political parties.

It is important to note, however, that the elections in Brazil are still largely controlled by economic power, which has compromised representation. The concentration of election campaign financing in the hands of ever fewer companies is increasing at the same frantic pace of cost increase. Between 2002 and 2010, there was an astonishing 600 per cent increase in the cost of electoral campaigns. In the 2010 elections, 1 per cent of donors contributed 61 per cent of total contributions and 10 of them with 22 per cent. A revealing piece of data indicates that the contributions were made by a small group that corresponds to 0.5 per cent of Brazilian companies (Sarmento & Osorio, 2014). Moreover, the relation between the financing of election campaigns and the election result is quite clear: among the 594 members of Congress (513 deputies and 81 senators) elected in 2010, 273 are businesspersons, 160 are large farmers and only 91 are considered to be representatives of workers (DIAP, 2013).

Similarly, the very few tools of public participation established by the 1988 Constitution have proved ineffective. The holding of referendums subject to prior authorisation by Congress and the submission of bills by the people are surrounded by so many requirements that have become virtually impossible. In the social sphere, the current Constitution has meant significant progress in labour and social security rights, having built a more egalitarian and universal social safety net. The 1988 Constitution was also innovative in relation to minorities, with the introduction of severe penalties for discrimination against women and afro-descendants.

Nonetheless, given the social and political context in which the country reconstitutionalisation was processed, the new was doomed to live with the old. This was the case of the centuries-old agrarian problem, which remained almost untouched, and of the military, which maintained their prerogative to intervene if requested by one of the three powers in the event of a serious political crisis.

The 1989 election, when 72 million voters went to the polls to elect the president, finally put an end to the transition's last phase (Kinzo, 2001). The inauguration of President-elect Fernando Collor de Mello marked symbolically the end of the long and complicated democratisation process. Yet, political developments would show that the re-emerging democracy would still have to go through various tests.

The drastic economic measures decreed by Collor the day after his inauguration, despite the radicalism with which they interfered arbitrarily in people's savings and investments and promoted wide trade liberalisation, soon proved ineffective to contain the crisis, leading to rapid erosion in popular support of the first president elected by direct vote. Serious allegations of corruption, followed by an impressive popular mobilisation led to Collor's impeachment in 1992 and the rise to the presidency of Vice-president Itamar Franco.

Franco's vacillating leadership initially contributed to worsening political and economic uncertainty in Brazil. However, the Real Plan, deployed a little later in his government, finally brought economic stability to the country. Political stability would come with the election of its architect, Fernando Henrique Cardoso (Party of Brazilian Social Democracy (PSDB)).

The Cardoso government (1995–98, 1999–2003) inaugurated an era of economic and political stability, combined with significant decline of social inequality, which lasted until the end of the Luiz Inácio Lula da Silva government (PT, 2003–6, 2007–11). During this 'Cardoso–Lula era', the axis of national politics turned on the competition between the PSDB and allies versus the PT and allies. Under such a 'bicoalitional architecture' (Power, 2010), several key policy domains were the object of consensus between the two camps, which, coupled with favourable external conditions, led to major economic and social advances in Brazil.

Concerning the economy, the current democratic regime had a cracking start, with a gross domestic product (GDP) annual growth in the range of 7–8 per cent for 1985 and 1986. However, the period also recorded increased inflation and currency devaluation, and late 1986 ushered in a long period of stagflation. The worst period extended from 1987 to 1992, during which the average GDP growth was negative (−0.14 per cent) and hyperinflation spiralled out of control, averaging 1300 per cent a year and jumping to nearly 2500 per cent in 1993 (Power, 2010).

Nevertheless, after the Real Plan ended hyperinflation and instituted a fiscal adjustment, Brazil grew at an average annual rate of 3.2 per cent between 1994 and 2008, far from the period 1930–80, when the average growth was 7 per cent a year, but still quite respectable. Inflation from 1995 to 2008 averaged only 8 per cent annually, a rate equivalent to three days of inflation in the final month of the Sarney government in 1990 (Power, 2010). The economic performance since the Real Plan until recently, although clearly uneven, can be characterised as moderate growth with low inflation.

From 1995 to 2002, the PT led the leftist faction in Congress, which vociferously and almost unanimously opposed all of the major Cardoso reforms. However, in his fourth race for the presidency, Lula released the Letter to the Brazilian People in June 2002, in which he pledged to leave most reforms intact and maintain the basic lines of Cardoso macroeconomic policy, a commitment that he hurried to meet as soon as he took office in January 2003. Of course, there were clear differences between the policies of Lula and those of his predecessor. Nonetheless, a consensus was formed around the ideas of continued inflation targeting, fiscal responsibility with a primary surplus, and monetary policy in defence of the new currency.

Social indicators also improved considerably in the Cardoso–Lula era. Democratisation coincided with increasing social inequality, with the Gini coefficient reaching 0.635 during the hyperinflation of 1989. Nevertheless, the Gini had been falling more or less steadily since the mid-1990s. The end of high inflation may explain the initial decline (inflation functioning as a de facto tax on the poor), but the trend was reinforced above all by the social programmes of conditional cash transfer that the Lula government had aggressively deployed since 2003.

Another factor that cannot be ignored is the minimum wage policy that had been implemented since the Real Plan. Both Cardoso and Lula had been pursuing a consistent policy of wage rises above the inflation rate in such a way that the real minimum wage had been increasing year by year from 1994 to 2009. Indeed, at the end of 2009, the real minimum wage had more than doubled in value since the deployment of the Real Plan. Virtually no political actor in Brazil opposed the social policies of the Lula government, which consolidated and expanded the Cardoso government initiatives, which in their turn had been strongly influenced by the PT innovations at the subnational level. The result was a social safety net that provided a guaranteed income for over 12 million families, covering almost a quarter of the national population (Power, 2010).

The socio-economic changes of course were reflected in the political system, which, during the Cardoso–Lula era, showed signs of stabilisation in electoral volatility and presidential contest. Although the electoral volatility for the Chamber of Deputies was notoriously high in the early years of democracy, averaging 43 per cent in the first three election cycles, after 1994 it decreased dramatically, averaging 31 per cent over the next three cycles and falling to 27.6 per cent in 2006. Presidential politics, in its turn, began to exhibit features of a two-party system, a surprising phenomenon in a country with one of the most fragmented party systems in the world. The last six presidential races (1994, 1998, 2002, 2006, 2010 and 2014) were fought primarily between the same two parties: the PSDB of Cardoso and the PT of Lula. In 2006, the PT and the PSDB jointly received 90.3 per cent of the vote in the first round of the presidential race (Power, 2010).

Obviously, the accommodation of multiple parties around these two major poles has not solved all the problems of a complex political arrangement that combines presidentialism as government system, federalism as a relation formula between the national and subnational powers, coalition as a governance formula (Abranches, 1988), and a fragmented party system, poorly institutionalised and highly regionalised (Abrucio, 1998). After all, although the multiple parties are quite similar to each other and vote as if they were large coalitions, the fact is that, when negotiating the vote, they behave as distinct actors. Thus, the situation that remains is that of a fragmented power game (Pinto, 2011, 2015).

It is so much so that during the Dilma Rousseff government (PT) – Lula's protégée, elected in 2010 and re-elected in 2014 owing to Lula's political capital, and temporarily removed from office while the Senate considers the accusation that she would have violated the budget laws thus causing fiscal imbalance – this 'implicit cross-party consensus' was broken. Such break-up, of course, was due to multiple factors, among which are macroeconomic policy change in a context of global economic crisis and Rousseff's evident inability to manage the political system or the so-called 'coalition presidentialism', problems that have been exacerbated by a huge corruption scandal involving all major political parties, both government and opposition. Besides having formed a larger and more heterogeneous coalition than her predecessors, Rousseff excessively concentrated power in a single party, hers.

Nevertheless, and despite the greater importance given to Congress by the 1988 Constitution in the decision-making process, in most of the post-1985 period the success rate of presidential initiatives[5] and their dominance rate on law production[6] have been incomparably higher than in the previous democratic period (1946–64), maintaining the heads of the Executive their leading role in defining public policies in Brazil. The success rate in the post-1988 period was 70.7 per cent, while in the 1949–64 period it was a meagre 29.5 per cent. Dominance rate for the post-1988 period is also significant: 85.6 per cent. In the previous democratic period, only 39 per cent of laws enacted were presidential initiatives (Limongi, 2006).

This may be partly explained by the fact that the 1988 Constitution has kept in the presidents' hands powerful legislative tools that had been granted under authoritarian regimes, such as: issuance of provisional measures with legal force – surrogate of the decree-laws introduced by Vargas and reintroduced by the military; exclusive initiative of major laws, including the budgetary laws – introduced by Vargas, maintained by the democratic regime of the period 1946–64, considerably enlarged by the military and to that extent maintained by the current regime; initiative to amend the Constitution – introduced by Vargas and reintroduced by the military; and prerogative to determine that bills be examined urgently by Congress – introduced by the military regime (Pinto, 2009).

Presidents also have powerful tools to intervene in the legislative process of budget approval, which enable them to establish and maintain public policy priorities. Similarly, presidents have considerable discretion in implementing the budget, which puts them in a privileged position to run government programmes that are part of their political agenda. At the end of the day, Congress action is restricted to specifying the application site of a small portion of the budget funds in strict accordance with policies considered priorities by the president (Figueiredo & Limongi, 2008).

Nonetheless, one of the most crucial explanations for the success of the post-1988 presidents in imposing a more progressive agenda on a Congress persistently and predominantly more conservative may be found in recent evidence set forth by the so-called Car Wash operation. A task force formed by Federal Police and Federal Revenue Service agents, as well as federal prosecutors, has turned into legal proof what has always been known in Brazil: a huge amount of public money has been misappropriated by members of successive governments, through private companies providing services to the state, to buy Congress support.

This may explain even the failure of the Dilma Rousseff government. From the moment that this huge corruption scheme began being investigated and the first politicians, civil servants and businesspersons began to be prosecuted and convicted, the money that irrigated the 'coalition presidentialism' also began to wane. The discussion on this dangerous proximity between coalition presidentialism (institutional framework within which the Brazilian Legislative and Executive relate to each other) and criminal underworld ushers in another important point of the argument: the judicialisation of politics.

The Brazilian Supreme Court, created at the dawn of the Republic and composed of 11 ministers appointed by the president upon Senate approval, was another institution empowered by the Constitution of 1988. Its power is such that today it is considered heir to the Moderating Power of the monarchical period, a position until recently attributed to the armed forces. Recently, the Supreme Court ordered the arrest of a senator and the temporary removal of the Chamber of Deputies' president, both of them for attempted obstruction of justice. These unprecedented decisions clearly go against the letter of the Constitution, which does not provide for temporary removal of houses of Congress presidents, or admit the arrest of their members except in flagrante delicto of a non-bailable offence (Pinto, 2009).

The Supreme Court not only controls the constitutionality of laws enacted in the country, eliminating from the legal world those laws that it considers unconstitutional, but also controls the very drafting of laws inside the houses of Congress. More than that, the Supreme Court has not limited itself simply to act as a negative lawmaker, abolishing the laws, wholly or partially, which it considers contrary to the Constitution, but it has also supplied alleged legislative gaps or lawmakers' omissions, acting in place of the Legislature, behaving, therefore, as a true positive policy-maker. One example is enough. One member of the Supreme Court, to justify convening a public hearing to discuss the More Doctors programme, instituted by a provisional measure issued by President Dilma Rousseff in 2013, made it clear the eminently political character of the activity: 'I shall clarify that [the] objective is to analyse, from the systemic point of view, the advantages and disadvantages of this public policy' (Oliveira, 2013).

This phenomenon of judicialisation of politics and social life seems to be part of a larger phenomenon of 'technicisation' of politics and social life seen throughout the Western or Westernised world. The most notable expressions of this larger phenomenon in Brazil were observed during the post-1964 authoritarian regime, when, in reaction to the populism tagged on the previous regime, the military carried out a depoliticisation of the state, replacing politicians by technocrats.

Recent manifestations of this phenomenon of depoliticising politics can be seen in the speeches of the current interim president, Michel Temer (PMDB), vice-president and Dilma Rousseff's former ally who influenced the group of Congress members who temporarily ousted her from the presidency. Temer announced that he would lead a government of 'national salvation' characterised by 'order and progress', and promised that his government would deploy an 'efficient democracy' guided by meritocracy. In just one month of the interim government, three members of Temer's 'ministry of notables' had to step down as new evidence produced by the Car Wash operation revealed their involvement in corruption. Indeed, the evidence produced by the Federal Police and by the Attorney General points out that these and other of Temer's allies triggered Rousseff's impeachment process as they considered that she was not being efficient enough to prevent the Car Wash operation from advancing.

In not just the 'technicisation' or depoliticisation of politics does the Temer interim government resemble the post-1964 military regime. They are also similar in trying to reverse the social gains achieved by the popular classes in the immediately preceding periods, with the clear intention to transfer more wealth to the top of the social pyramid occupied by an elite segment fully integrated into the capitalist world-economy. Temer and his economic team have announced drastic measures to reduce public spending on health, education and social security, and prevent minimum wage rises above the inflation rate. That is, just like the military, Temer wants to reverse the previous social-democratic governments' policy of a steady increase in the purchasing power of the popular and working classes.

Nonetheless, there is another actor that has been continuously gaining momentum and has the power to break the continuous cycle of intra-elite struggle between a nationalist-developmentalist segment and an internationalist segment that, directly or indirectly, has appropriated the Brazilian state and its institutions: the people.

As can be seen in the narrative of the history of Brazilian politics constructed in this paper, the mass of individuals in Brazil has been left out not only in the sharing of national material and cultural wealth, but also of the major political decision-making processes. In fact, it is only after the 1930 Revolution that one begins to notice some popular expressions of a clearly political character. Yet, it was not until the late 1960s and early 1970s, in the wake of the 1968 World Revolution, that larger numbers of Brazilians took to the streets of major cities to protest against a sham democracy and require a wider inclusion, not only political but also socio-economic. In 1984, the PMDB and other opposition parties to the military government managed to bring millions of people to the streets across the country to demand direct elections for president in what was hitherto considered the largest popular demonstration in the history of Brazil. In 1992, a slightly smaller number of people, mostly young students, took to the streets to demand the impeachment of President Collor.

Since June 2013, however, an entirely new political phenomenon has occurred in Brazil: millions of people have been occupying the streets and public squares across the country, in a sequence and quantity without any precedent in the history of Brazilian politics. These mass protests, which initially demanded more and better public services, especially more and better infrastructure for urban mobility, have evolved into protests against excessive privileges and pervasive corruption of politicians, as well as against and in favour of the Rousseff government.

This sequence of huge protests has in common a wide and deep disenchantment with representative democracy, an aspect in which they resemble the mass protests that, since December 2010, have broken out in different regions around the world. The vast majority of these global protests, each in its own way, has shown intolerance with increasing privileges of small minorities translated into never fulfilled promises of economic prosperity and political participation. These new global social movements share, among other things, the struggle for the communal. They want to replace the economic growth goal by the maximum decommodification goal, which Native American movements call 'buen viver'. This means not only resist the increasing drive for commodification of the last 30 years – education, health, body, water and air – but also decommodification of agricultural and industrial production (Pinto, Guimarães, & Barros, 2016).

More than that, the new global social movements have questioned the very structures of political representation and liberal governance regimes. The audacious leap made by the theory and practice of representative democracy – from the 'will of all' towards the 'general will' – finally proved fatal, and even new forms of governance, extended as a safety net to the falling acrobat, have proved to be excessively worn and fragile.

Conclusion

This paper has interpreted the major political events in Brazil's history and constructed a narrative according to which the history of Brazilian politics is marked much more by continuities than by discontinuities. The nearly two centuries of Brazil's existence as an independent state may be – in general terms and at the risk of overgeneralisation – characterised as an economic and political intra-elite dispute between an internationalist segment, more integrated into the capitalist world-system, and a segment more nationalist, more interested in the development of the domestic industry and consumer market.

The elite internationalist segment, in its successive configurations – raw materials export and manufactured goods import, industry associated with foreign capital, and rentism – clearly has prevailed most of the time, and the Brazilian state and its institutions have been shaped to suit its interests. The nationalist-developmentalist segment, in turn, predominated in only two periods of Brazilian politics: the Vargas or populist period, both in its authoritarian (1930–34, 1937–45) and democratic (1946–64) phases, and the Cardoso–Lula–Rousseff or social-democrat period (1995–2014) – despite having been labelled as 'the homeland peddler' for his privatisation policy, Cardoso implemented it half-heartedly, a process that Lula did not reverse; Rousseff deployed a private provision of public services policy that differs little from Cardoso's privatisation policy.

Throughout almost two centuries, although it has adopted and maintained the main ideals, institutions and procedures of liberal democracy, even during the post-1964 military dictatorship, Brazil has done it most of the time only formally, so that with rare exceptions what has been seen in the country is a democracy without 'demos' (people) and a respublica with no 'public'. Thus, for most of the history of Brazilian politics, the majority of the population has been left outside the sharing of national resources, both material and cultural, and has been kept out of the most important political decision-making processes.

For most of the time, elections have functioned more as a means of social control than as a truly democratic instrument of formation of the people's representative bodies. Far from actually representing the Brazilian people in all its plurality, over time the Legislative has served to legitimise the elite's different segments that have alternated in power, revealing a more conservative profile than the society at large and even than most of the successive heads of the Executive.

Congress's more conservative profile, secured by the institutional arrangement that has been maintained in the country, has allowed presidents a more important role in the public policy-making process, with legislatures behaving sometimes as a collaborator, sometimes as a saboteur of the heads of the Executive's initiatives. It has been observed in the narrative of the history of Brazilian politics constructed in this paper that both before and after the 1988 Constitution, the Legislative has played a secondary role, as compared with the Executive, in the process of defining public policies in the country, a position it has been forced to share with another increasingly important actor: the Supreme Court. In the wake of the global phenomenon of technicisation of politics and social life, the judiciary, the most technical of the state organs, increasingly acts as lawgiver not only negatively, by removing from the legal world those laws it deems unconstitutional, but also positively, acting in place of the Legislative in defining public policies.

Another actor, however, that for a long time had been kept behind the scenes, forces its way into the spotlight: the people. Since June 2013, millions of Brazilians have gone on to the streets on several occasions, and there is no evidence that this popular rising will cool down. Notwithstanding the varied list of demands, a theme pervades these multiple and biggest protests ever seen in the history of Brazilian politics: the majority of the population, not only the lower classes, but also the middle classes, do not perceive themselves as being represented in countless political parties and in Congress.

In this state of affairs, if Congress wants to effectively function as a privileged public space in which government, opposition, social and environmental movement organisations, and other entities representing multiple segments of society gather to discuss and define public policy, it will have to become more transparent and permeable to popular participation and control, and reform the political system in order to ensure proportional representation of all segments of society, overcoming the representation deficit of women, afro-descendants and other social minorities, and the surplus economic influence on politics.

Briefly, the solution to the crisis of representation, more representation and participation, is the radicalisation or democratisation of democracy.

Notes

1. Public policies are understood in this paper as the set of programmes, actions and activities developed directly or indirectly by the state, with the participation of public and private entities, which aim at ensuring certain rights of citizenship.
2. The State Council, according to the Constitution of 1824, alleviated the irresponsibility of the Emperor. The Moderating Power was exerted, except in the case of appointment and dismissal of ministers, upon the hearing of that

body. Often it served to justify the Sovereign, compromising the powerful ones in his decisions. It was for this reason that the liberals wanted to put it out together with the Moderating Power.

3. The Brazilian Communist Party (PCB) was outlawed in 1947. Although some of its members were able to be elected by other parties, and had leaders in unions, magazines and weeklies, the PCB could not hold meetings except clandestinely and under permanent police repression. The absence of ideological and party pluralism in the pre-1964 period constituted therefore a serious distortion of political democracy in the country.

4. This paper considers the José Sarney government (1985–89) to be the last phase of the transition from dictatorship to democracy.

5. The proportion of what is approved over what is sent to Congress by the president.

6. Simple division of laws derived from the president's initiative by the total of laws enacted in the period.

Disclosure statement

No potential conflict of interest was reported by the author.

References

Abranches, S. H. (1988). Presidencialismo de coalizão: o dilema institucional brasileiro. *Dados, 31*(1), 5–33.

Abrucio, F. L. (1998). *Os Barões da Federação: os governadores e a redemocratização brasileira*. São Paulo: Hucitec/USP.

Cardoso, F. H. (1993). *O modelo político brasileiro*. Rio de Janeiro: Bertrand Brasil.

Carvalho, J. M. (2013). *Cidadania no Brasil: o longo caminho*. Rio de Janeiro: Civilização Brasileira.

Codato, A. N. (2005). Uma história política da transição brasileira: da ditadura militar à democracia. *Revista de Sociologia Política, Curitiba, 25*, 83–106.

Departamento Intersindical de Assessoria Parlamentar (DIAP). (2013). *Reforma política e regime representativo*. Retrieved from http://www.diap.org.br/index.php?option=com_jdownloads&Itemid=513&view=finish&cid=396&catid=83.

Dreifuss, R. A., & Dulci, O. S. (2008). As forças armadas e a política. In B. Sorj & M. H. T. Almeida (Eds.), *Sociedade política no Brasil pós-61* (pp. 132–181). Rio de Janeiro: Centro Edelstein de Pesquisas Sociais.

Faoro, R. (2012). *Os donos do poder: formação do patronato político brasileiro*. São Paulo: Editora Globo.

Figueiredo, A. C., & Limongi, F. M. P. (2008). *Política orçamentária no presidencialismo de coalizão*. Rio de Janeiro: Editora FGV.

Ianni, O. (1988). *O colapso do populismo no Brasil.* Rio de Janeiro: Civilização Brasileira.

Kinzo, M. D. G. (2001). A democratização brasileira: um balanço do processo político desde a transição. *São Paulo em Perspectiva, 15*(4), 3–12.

Limongi, F. (2006). Democracia no Brasil: presidencialismo, coalizão partidária e processo decisório. *Novos Estudos - CEBRAP, 76,* 17–41.

Oliveira, M. (2013). Supremo fará audiência pública antes de julgar Mais Médicos. *G1.* Retrieved from http://g1.globo.com/bemestar/noticia/2013/10/supremo-fara-audiencia-publica-antes-de-julgar-mais-medicos.html.

Pinto, J. R. S. (2009). *Poder Legislativo brasileiro: institutos e processos.* Rio de Janeiro: Editora Forense.

Pinto, J. R. S. (2011). *Sistema político e comportamento parlamentar.* Brasília: Editora Consulex.

Pinto, J. R. S. (2015). Entre um sistema eleitoral dispersivo e um regramento parlamentar concentrador: o comportamento dos deputados federais. *Revista Direito GV, 11*(2), 589–622.

Pinto, J. R. S., Guimarães, D. M., & Barros, F. L. (2016). A crise da democracia representativa. *E-Legis, 9*(19), 39–48.

Power, T. J. (2010). Brazilian democracy as a late bloomer: Reevaluating the regime in the Cardoso-Lula era. *Latin American Research Review, 45*(Special Issue), 218–247.

Santos, W. G. (1987). *Cidadania e justiça: a política social na ordem brasileira.* Rio de Janeiro: Campus.

Sarmento, D., & Osorio, A. (2014). Uma mistura tóxica: política, dinheiro e financiamento das eleições. Retrieved from http://www.migalhas.com.br/arquivos/2014/1/art20140130-01.pdf

Souza, P. H. G. P., & Medeiros, M. (2015). Top income shares and inequality in Brazil, 1928-2012. *Journal of the Brazilian Sociological Society, 1*(1), 119–132.

Toledo, C. N. (2004). 1964: o golpe contra as reformas e a democracia. *Revista Brasileira de História, 24*(47), 13–28.

The role of the Brazilian Congress in defining public social policies

Fábio de Barros Correia Gomes ⒾⒹ and
Ricardo Chaves de Rezende Martins ⒾⒹ

ABSTRACT
The analysis of the role of Congress in defining public policy matters to the debate on the characterisation of legislatures in a spectrum that ranges from the 'transformative' to the 'arena' type (according to the typology of Polsby). This paper, related to the Brazilian case, considers definitions relevant to the areas of education and health. On education, this study presents an analysis of the content of the legislative proposals of parliamentarians and two case studies, which discuss policy definitions of funding and quality assessment. On health, this article presents an analysis of related legislative proposals and especially those that resulted in funding rules. These studies suggest that Congress in Brazil has an important part to play in defining public policies, acting either as a transforming agent or as an arena for debates. The Brazilian Congress seems to have been, at the same time, active, reactive, collaborative and innovative. This finding leads to the conclusion that the Brazilian Legislature must be placed at an intermediate level between the extreme types of Polsby's categories; this position is compatible with the 'coalitional presidentialism'.

Introduction

In the context of contemporary Brazilian democracy, how can we more precisely characterise the role of the Federal Legislative Branch, the National Congress, in the formulation of the normative outlines of the public policies? The answer to this question is relevant since the specialised literature frequently grants to the Brazilian Legislative Branch a mere reactive or confirming role, facing an Executive Branch endowed with a wide range of power to initiate legislation or to influence the legislative process.

According to several authors, the peculiarities existing in the relationships between the Executive and Legislative Branches of the Brazilian government, the distribution of competences and legislative attributions established by the Constitution suggest that the former, who detains a power of agenda-making in several crucial matters for the organisation of public administration and social life in general, seems to be dominant, submitting the latter branch to a secondary role (Moisés, 2011; Pereira & Mueller, 2000).

In fact, the Brazilian Constitution bestows on the Executive Branch a wide range of legislative attributions. Of its exclusive prerogative, are, for example, laws about the manpower of the Army, creation of agencies and roles in public administration, and, especially, budgetary laws. The president of the Republic also has powers to request urgency in the approval of law projects. His greater power, however, lies in editing provisory measures, with force of law, in case of urgency and relevance. These acts have immediate validity and are to be appraised by the National Congress in due time.

The significant means of legislative initiative and acceleration of the legislative process to the disposal of the Executive Branch seem to grant it an extraordinary preponderance in defining public policies.

On the other hand, despite these powers of legislative initiative that the Constitution assures to the Executive Branch, a need actually to approve matters in the legislative arena still remains.[1] In a multiparty regime (Brazil boasts more than 20 political parties with representation in the National Congress) the president of the Republic needs to create broad and diverse parliamentary coalitions. This results in the Executive Branch establishing division of its administrative powers among the political parties in such a way as to assure the necessary support during votes at the legislative houses, be it through formal means, such as the sharing of office positions (for example, when composing a coalition Minister Office), or through various negotiations of different nature, characterising a coalition presidentialism (Abranches, 1988). Thus, the production of public policies in Brazil depends on interaction between members of the Executive and Legislative Branches, who share the power, according to limits and possibilities of action established based on constitutional, legal and regimental rules (of the legislative houses).

Some empirical studies have questioned the above-mentioned predominance of the Executive Branch in legislative production. Cruz (2009) and Amaral (2009) have pointed to the relevance of the Legislative in changing proposals that come from the Executive Branch. Ricci (2003) indicated that the Legislative Branch is not an impeditive space for the implementation of innovative policies and that its interventions would not always result in proposals that were tainted by the dominance of particular interests, unlike suggested by Mainwaring (1999) and Ames (2003).

An analysis of the legislative production of the National Congress based on the 21,000 proposals introduced between 1999 and 2006 indicated that the Executive ranked highest as the author of ordinary laws, but not when it came to more highly regarded norms, such as complementary laws and amendments to the Constitution (Gomes, 2011). However, members of the government coalition were the authors of 90 per cent of the proposals that were converted into legal norms both in the ordinary and constitutional paths.

The influence of the Legislature in the formation of public policies was emphasised in labour (Vogel, 2010), economic (Braga, 2011) and educational (Martins, 2012) studies. In regards to health policies, some studies emphasised the preponderance of the Executive in the approval of laws in the post-constitutional period (Baptista, 2003, 2010; Rodrigues & Zauli, 2002); others pointed to a predominance of the Legislature in the approval of ordinary laws and constitutional amendments (Godoi, 2008; Gomes, 2011).

So, despite the apparent lack of balance in favour of the Executive Branch, does the need to ensure governability make the relationship between the two branches of the Republic less asymmetrical? In this scenario, is it possible to position or frame the Legislature in the traditionally adopted typologies to characterise the institution? Is it feasible to place the Brazilian Parliament in the continuum between 'transformative legislature' and 'arena legislature', as proposed by the Polsby (1975) typology? Or is it feasible to classify it as 'active', 'reactive' or 'labeller', as suggested by Santos (2004)?

Although the answer to these questions requires the analysis of a range of dimensions, studying the action of the Legislature in the scope of normatisation of public policies might generate a relevant contribution to its understanding.

This work contemplates case studies in two policy fields: education and health. We examine the contribution of the Legislative Branch in the elaboration of norms regarding funding and evaluation of education and funding of health.[2]

The cases consider situations where the analysed policy is part of the proposal agenda of the Executive (in the case of education), as well as those where this branch resists the adoption of politics (health).[3] We devoted special attention to the capacity of the Legislature to cooperate in the creation and also to modify substantially the production of policies in the areas analysed.

In education, we discuss the performance of the Legislative Branch from two focuses. Initially, we analyse, for the period from 1995 to 2006, the set of initiatives of educational law projects, authored by deputies, to identify the degree and the subjects of interest of the parliamentarians in this public policy area. Then, we examine the performance of the Legislative Branch in two important legislative modifications in the same period: the redefinition of funding policies for basic education and the evaluation of higher education. Later, we analyse this performance in the area of health. We present syntheses about the introduction of proposals about health (in general) in the National Congress between 1999 and 2006 and about the course of relevant legislative proposals for the definition of funding for the national public health system, the Sistema Único de Saúde (SUS), with a focus on the relationship between actors from the Legislative and Executive Branches in the post-Constitution period of 1988.

In the final considerations, in light of the cases examined, we identify the performance profile of the Legislative Branch in the definition of these public policies, emphasising a significant role that is not frequently highlighted in the political science literature of the country.

The performance of the Chamber of Deputies in educational matters

The systematic analysis of the contribution of the National Congress to the definition of recent structural policies of national education contradicts the publicised thesis that the role of the Legislature is secondary or merely ratifying. There is a distinguished degree of participation of the Legislature in the formulation of public policies.

This substantiation results from research about the performance of the Legislative Branch in three legislatures (1995–99, 1999–2003 and 2003–7), contemplating the analysis of the propositions presented by the deputies in the education field and an in-depth study of structural changes in the legal order of educational funding and evaluation of higher education. In the case of educational funding, we studied the course and approval of two constitutional amendments (in 1996 and 2006, respectively), which introduced important systems for the redistribution of resources between the federal units. With regards to higher education, we discuss the legislation about the institution of a national system of evaluation, in 1995, and its modification, in 2004.

Law project initiatives of parliamentarians in the educational area

The research showed that parliamentary initiatives were primarily regarding general policies with diffuse costs and benefits, especially those linked to funding and organisation of education. Also present, but on a much smaller scale, were proposals with diffuse costs for the distribution of localised benefits, such as, for example, proposals for the creation of federal schools located at the electoral focus of parliamentarians. Table 1 presents the distribution of these parliamentary initiatives by subject.

These findings confirm what other studies in the national scenario had already demonstrated. Parliamentarians, in their initiatives for education, are more oriented to wide issues of public policies than to the satisfaction of particular or 'parish' interests (Figueiredo & Limongi, 1996; Lemos, 2001; Ricci & Lemos, 2004; Ricci, 2003).

The number of projects proposed by the parliamentarians was impressive, even with the knowledge that most of these proposals end their days in an archive. Through time, the number of projects about educational matters has

grown in the same proportion as the elevation of the total number of proposals of this type presented to the Chamber of Deputies. A considerable
proportion (43 per cent) of the deputies that carried out, partially or
totally, their terms between 1995 and 2007, presented at least one law
project regarding education. The data collected, therefore, have shown that
public educational policies constitute an area of significant legislative interest
for the deputies.

The amount of proposals about the subject, between 7 and 9 per cent in the
universe of law projects presented in each legislature (on average, 493 projects
on education over a total of 6711 law projects) during the period considered,
confirms the social appeal of educational issues in the parliamentary environment. This finding is true for parties with larger or smaller benches (40–55 per
cent of the parliamentarians, in each party, independently of the size of their
bench, presented at least one law project for education). It is still valid if the
party was with the government or opposed the Executive Branch (the average
number of law projects in education by bench for the Brazilian Social-Democ-
racy Party (PSDB) and Worker's Party (PT), parties of the presidents of the
Republic of the period, tended to even out throughout the period).

Regarding the political-ideological dimension, we observed a greater presence of initiatives in the educational area among parties of the left (49 per cent
of parliamentarians of their benches with educational law projects, compared
with 40 per cent in the parties placed in the remaining positions of the range).
This is shown in Table 2.

Also, when the specific content of the proposals for the amendment of the
Constitution was analysed, in educational funding a distinction between the
centre and left parties, on one side, and of the right parties, on the other
was revealed. The former were more oriented towards basic public education
and the right-wing ones to private funding of education.

Still in regard to these larger subjects, the legislative behaviour of the deputies while presenting initiatives does not seem to be substantially different, in
the political party environment, in accordance with them having changed

Table 1. Number of law projects in education by parliamentary initiative, according to
the subject: 1995–2006.

Subject of the law projects	Number of law projects	%
Educational funding (especially public education)	497	34
General education organisational norms	296	20
Curriculum	181	12
Creation of federal schools in towns	171	11
Supplementary educational support programmes (school transportation, school nutrition, school material and health assistance)	162	11
Other subjects	172	12
Total:	1479	100

Source: SILEG – Chamber of Deputies.

positions in relation to the Executive Branch. However, when examining the subject of educational funding, the data found suggest the existence of a relationship between the position of the party, as incumbent or opposition, and the thematic subgroup of the projects presented by the parliamentarians. In fact, when one party was occupying the Executive Branch, we verified a tendency towards the presentation of a larger proportion of projects towards general funding policies. When this party was opposing the Executive, the percentage of projects concerning policies/instruments for attending to specific audiences or individuals was preponderant. These initiatives have, in general, a larger direct impact with people, that is, the electors, providing more visibility to the parliamentarians. They concern, in general, scholarship programmes for certain social groups, fiscal exemptions for certain educational expenses that reach certain strata of the society and benefits for students of a certain social origin, etc.

Regarding proposals for amendments to the Constitution, we verified that, when in office, both political parties (PSDB and PT) tended to display a greater legislative will to intervene in issues concerning educational funding. As government parties, about 60 per cent of the proposals for constitutional amendments presented by parliamentarians concerned this subject. When opposing, the participation of initiatives for norms for general organisation of education increased to more than 50 per cent, related to the affirmation of diffuse citizenship rights and generic duties of public power. This, in a certain way, contradicts an expectation that the parties, once they become part of government, would leave to the Executive Branch the incumbency of defining the more structuring policies, such as the ones that deal with educational funding.

Educational laws approved in the period between 1995 and 2010

When examining the cases of educational laws that came into effect in the period between 1995 and 2010, the analysed data show a significant intervention by the Legislative Branch in the definition of educational public policies, even though the initiative of the proposals originated, in

Table 2. Proportion of deputies who presented law projects for the educational area in the total of benches of their parties, according to their placement in the ideological-political range: 1995–2006.

Political-ideological orientation of the party	Proportion of deputies who present law projects for education (%)
Right	39
Centre	40
Left	49

Source: SILEG – Chamber of Deputies.

great part, in the Executive Branch. The National Congress modified a portion of the proposals sent by the president of the Republic. These data are shown in Table 3.

We verified that the initiative in itself cannot be taken as a representation of the entire legislative process or of the result that morphs into legal norm. The degree of intervention of the Legislative Branch in the review of law projects and temporary measures edited by the president of the Republic, for example, was high. Of the 61 published laws, 33 originated from an initiative of the Executive Branch. However, among those, less than one-third (10) was approved by the National Congress in its original version; 19 became law based on substitutions presented to the Legislative Branch (significantly modifying its contents) and four received substantial amendments. Thus, although the Executive Branch has exerted its power of initiative in educational laws, the Legislative Branch has performed relevantly in the appreciation of proposals, amending them and also deeply altering them, contributing greatly to the final formulation of the educational legislation.

Even without exerting an original role in the conception of innovative public policies, the Legislative Branch intervened significantly in its ultimate definition, through the mechanisms of amendment and negotiation. Recurrently, the final content of the examined laws was substantially different from the projects that were originally submitted. The Brazilian Congress was not an obstacle to innovation in structural educational policies, but a collaborative and participative agent. On the other hand, it has shown resistance to the limitation of social rights, in the educational area, guaranteed by the Constitution of 1988.

Table 3. Published educational laws, by type of originating proposal, according to originating branch and degree of modification of the original text by the Legislative Branch: 1995–2010.

Period/type Source/text	Executive Branch				Legislative Branch			
	Total	OR*	AM*	SUB*	Total	OR*	AM*	SUB*
1995–2002								
Temporary measures	6	2	2	2	–	–	–	–
Law projects	10	3	4	3	12	2	3	7
Total:	16	5	6	5	12	2	3	7
2003–10								
Temporary measures	13	1	–	12	–	–	–	–
Law projects	20	9	4	7	28	9	12	7
Total:	33	10	4	19	28	9	12	7

Note: * OR = original text approved without modifications; AM = text approved with amendments; SUB = text approved in the form of substitutive. Regarding temporary measures, if the law project for conversion encompassed less significant amendments, it was sorted as 'AM', that is, text approved with amendments; if the law project for conversion significantly altered the content of the original text, it was classified as 'SUB', that is, text approved in the form of substitutive.
Source: SILEG – Chamber of Deputies.

The data indicated that, during the period, the legislative agenda in the educational area was shared between the two branches and the proposals of the president of the Republic were widely discussed, negotiated and modified in the National Congress. We observed the fact that the presidents resorted to the use of temporary measures, which, despite their impact in the course of matters of their interest, did not mean that they got their proposals approved as originally presented.

The case studies about funding of education and evaluation of higher education

Case studies were also conducted, deepening two strategic fields of educational public policies: education funding and evaluation of higher education. These cases have shown that, far from representing superficial modifications or simple adjustments without any major repercussions, the modifications made in the Legislative Branch characterised a decisive performance of this branch in the legal formulation of these politics, as we shall show.

The research covered the terms of the presidents of the Republic, bound to opposite political parties between them, covering the period from 1995 to 2007. From January 1995 to January 2003, two terms of President Fernando Henrique, of the PSDB, occurred. From January 2003 to January 2007, the first term of President Lula da Silva, of the PT, an opposition party to the previous president, occurred. Different governments, with diverse parliamentary supports, promoted radical changes in the funding mechanisms of public education, implementing procedures for redistributing resources and involving the three spheres of the Brazilian Federation. These initiatives constituted innovation in the educational public policies, establishing a new funding standard. Its discussion and approval in the National Congress revealed a relevant performance of the Legislative Branch in the definition of its legal outlines, as we shall demonstrate.

The modifications in the mechanisms for financing basic education required constitutional modifications, in which the Executive Branch saw the Legislative Branch approve the main content of its proposals for amendments to the Constitution (PEC), but with some differences. In the first case, proposed by President Fernando Henrique, in 1995,[4] the specific devices were approved practically as they were submitted to Congress, but at the expense of an abdication by the Executive Branch of a number of reforms simultaneously proposed for higher education and for children's education.[5] The government parties significantly altered the PEC in other subjects that are not specifically the funding of basic education, but without the relevant participation of the president's party.

Regarding the proposal of President Lula da Silva, the proposal for constitutional amendment,[6] presented in 2005, referred exclusively to the funding of basic education. It was also greatly altered, with an intense intervention of the president's supporting parties, especially his own party, which relies on a significant bench connected to public education interests. Besides that, after 10 years of effectiveness of the first constitutional change in the funding of basic education, the positions of the federal units and the educational entities of the civil society about the adopted model had certainly matured. Thus, if the first modification, which occurred in 1996, was mostly non-negotiated, the new change proposed in 2005 was subject to a lot of negotiation between the Legislature and Executive Branches, and the latter was led to agree with important changes proposed by parliamentarians. If their initial posture was to get the approval of legislation that would progressively release the federal government from responsibilities regarding basic education, the results, in the end, went in the opposite direction.

An analysis of the legislative case regarding the evaluation of higher education has shown a different process when compared with previous case studies.[7] The conclusions at which we arrived, however, were similar. The course of action and the changes introduced by the Legislative Branch constituted a space for negotiating and redevelopment of projects. These processes proved their competence in generating new consistent wordings, especially regarding the approval, in 2004, of a new evaluation system, in this case cooperating directly with the Executive Branch itself. Contradicting some affirmations that the Legislative Branch allegedly tends to distort or generate inconsistencies in the legislative diplomas, the possibility of producing legal texts that balance the diverse interests of all the parties involved, in the environment of the National Congress, seems to have been revealed. In the case we are commenting on, we also observed a contrary reaction of the Legislative Branch to delegate to the Executive Branch almost indiscriminate powers to fix public policy norms for the evaluation of higher education; therefore, a trend towards predicting, in the law, the general norms for public policies, stabilising them and making them less susceptible to harsh modifications by the sheer will of the governing officers. Again, we verify that the National Congress was not an obstacle to the implementation of innovative public policies, but collaborated with the Executive Branch.

During the polls, confirming the studies by Figueiredo and Limongi (1996), the parties were disciplined and consistent with their positioning in their relationship with the Executive Branch. There was, however, an intense negotiation process between the parties and the Legislative and Executive Branches, revealed by an examination of the entire course of the considered propositions.

Although studies of similar cases do not allow for generalisations, the conclusions of the analysis conducted might clarify or enrich the approaches to gauge the agenda power in the definition of the public policies by the number of approved proposals, depending on the initiative or source branch. It is a fact, in Brazil, that the vast majority of laws stems from proposals presented by the Executive Branch. In the case studies in question, all of the proposals were presented by this branch. However, the transformative action of Congress was significant in all of the projects, with two important policy inversions, one for each government period. The broad project for the educational reform of the Fernando Henrique government (1995–99, first term) was modified, with the changes practically restricted to the funding of elementary education and the necessary modifications to its implementation, such as the definition of the primordial responsibilities of the federal instances. Regarding the Lula da Silva government (2003–7, first term), the direction of the proposal for participation of the Union in the funding of basic education was inverted: from a progressive release to a continuous and proportional involvement through the whole life of Fundo de Manutenção e Desenvolvimento da Educação Básica e de Valorização dos Profissionais da Educação – FUNDEB.

The results we found show that the National Congress, in a crucial educational public policy issue, acted decisively to implement an important innovation in the funding of public education. The modifications introduced by the parliamentarians in the appreciated proposals resulted in consistent legal texts. These findings contradict affirmations, such as Ames (2003), that the Legislative Branch, with a greater number of veto players, is allegedly averse to significant changes to public policies and that the diverse interests of the parliamentarians, with their localised characteristics, would result in less consistent legislative texts.

We obtained similar findings to the ones formulated by Diniz (2005), that is, the Executive and Legislative Branches acted collaboratively, with allowances from the former and significant intervention from the latter, without any detriment to governability and to the introduction of the most relevant changes requested in the proposals that were judged and approved.

The most important finding is that, in the most structuring issues for educational public policies, normally submitted to the National Congress by the president of the Republic, the intervention of the Legislative Branch was meaningful, even leading to the approval of texts, in certain cases, with an opposing orientation in relation to the one originally intended by the Executive Branch. The resulting wordings have not expressed a pile of particularistic amendments, but reflected a broad negotiation along consensual lines of policy. They also revealed that the alternation of political parties in the Executive Branch has not broke these policies, but has allowed for a continuity and improvement or broadening of their scope.

Finally, we verified that the position of the benches in votes relating to structural issues of national education changed, through time, in light of their relationship with the Executive Branch (government or opposition).

This happened to the benefit of continuity and stability of the public policies for funding education and evaluating higher education. In fact, the case studies revealed that the party of the president that was inaugurated in 2003, once in power, took over legislative proposals that included dispositions that it had publicly spoke against while it was the opposing party. The party of the former president, in turn, probably by recognising some continuity in the proposals that were approved when they were in power, voted in favour of the proposals in both government periods. In fact, before the approval of the first change in the mechanism for financing elementary education (creation of the Fundo de Manutenção e Desenvolvimento do Ensino Fundamental e de Valorização do Magistério – FUNDEF), the PT opposed the proposal of the then president of the Republic, of the PSDB party. When proposing the expansion of this mechanism to the whole of basic education, the PT kept the same system, in 2006. The same happened in regard to the evaluation of higher education: the changes conducted in 2004, under the PT government, took advantage of the basis of the evaluation system proposed by the PSDB government, in 1995.

Legislature and health: health funding case

Health is an area that generates considerable interest in the performance of the National Congress. Table 4 indicates that, among all of the proposals that came into the Chamber of Deputies between 1999 and 2006 to modify or create legal rules, 25 per cent were related to health. In the legislative path that produces ordinary laws, the percentage was 29 per cent; in the path that produces complementary laws (by demand of the constitutional composition), it was 14 per cent; and in the path that results in amendments to the Constitution, 11 per cent. We would like to highlight that the members of the National Congress have written about 90 per cent of the proposals in all of the legislative paths (Gomes, 2011). Health is also at a forefront position among the proposals converted into legal regulations, linked to 15 per cent of the production in the aforementioned period (Table 4).

Table 4. Distribution of proposal subjects in all of the policy areas and in those related to health, that entered the Chamber between 1999 and 2006 and status of conversion into legal rule observed in March 2009.

	Proposal subject			
	All		Health	
Legislature paths	Introduced	Converted into rule	Introduced	Converted into rule
Constitutional	1646	21	178	9
Complementary	952	25	134	2
Ordinary	17,554	1699	5007	257
Total:	21,447	1745	5319	268

Source: Gomes (2011).

Table 5 shows a comparison between success and dominance rates[8] of selected authors, in different legislative paths of the National Congress, of proposals in all policy subjects and in those related to health. We observed that, in a grand pool of subjects, the success and dominance rates of the Executive Branch were inversely proportional to the hierarchical level of the legislative paths. This gradual progression has also occurred for all of the authors, but the levels of success of the Executive Branch were much superior. A quantitative dominance of the Executive has not occurred in the highest ranked path; however, a dominance of the coalition occurred in all of the paths, amounting to about 90 per cent of the ordinary and constitutional paths. These findings suggest that the system is geared towards the promotion of governability, particularly to the approval of policies in lower ranked paths.

For the whole pool of health-related proposals, the dominance rates of the Executive also behaved in an inverse proportion to the rank of the paths. However, this has not occurred in relation to the success rates, because of a better performance of the Executive Branch in the constitutional path than in the complementary path (Table 4). Even when considering the production of all of the authors, the constitutional path has obtained a much higher success rate when compared with the one obtained in the general pool of subjects, surpassing the rates of other paths, reflecting the fact that health is a 'constitutionalised' policy. As in the general pool of subjects, coalition has maintained its dominance in the production of constitutional and ordinary paths.

These data suggest that, both for health issues and for the general pool of proposals for all of the subjects, the members of the Legislature have been influencing relevant definitions about public policies. The qualitative synthesis, for the case presented below, points in the same direction.

Health funding

The Federal Constitution of 1988 established the SUS as universal (to serve all of the citizens) and structured as a regional and hierarchical network, under

Table 5. Distribution of success and dominance rates, according to legislative paths, of proposals in all of the policy subjects and in those related to health, from select authors, that entered the Chamber between 1999 and 2006, and course situation observed in March 2009.

Path	Success rates (%)				Dominance rates (%)			
	All authors		Executive		Executive		Coalition	
	AA	Health	AA	Health	AA	Health	AA	Health
Constitutional	1.3	6.1	36.8	66.7	33.3	44.4	90.5	88.9
Complementary	2.6	1.8	53.8	33.3	56.0	50.0	72.0	50.0
Ordinary	9.0	5.1	76.6	76.4	76.9	70.2	89.2	85.7

Source: Gomes (2011).
Note: AA = all policy areas.

guidelines aimed towards decentralisation, integrity of care and community participation. The system is to be funded with resources from the three levels of the government: federal, state and municipal.

According to Rodriguez Neto (2003), public health funding was one of the health subjects that was most controverted during the Constitutional Assembly of 1988, and, as a result of that, an 'indefinition' about a stable parameter for the funding of the area occurred. During this period, the private industry of health, on the one hand, and health professionals and civil society organisations (that constituted the 'sanitary reform movement') on the other, defended opposite positions (regarding the participation of the private and public sectors in health) through their representatives in the Legislature. The Executive Branch did not lead the discussion because of its vulnerability due to the context of redemocratisation. The result of the impasse was the creation of a mixed health system, basically public, but that allows for the participation of the private sector.

About health funding, a temporary solution was reached because a transitory disposition act indicated that, until the approval of the budgetary guideline law (each year), 30 per cent minimum of the social security budget, except for unemployment insurance, should be destined for health.

After the definitions of the Constitutional Assembly, the temporary funding criterion was maintained until 1994, when President Franco blocked the device in the Budgetary Guideline Law due to the serious financial crisis in social security. We should stress that, if this temporary criterion had been adopted as a permanent solution, federal resources for health would be double that obtained with the prevailing criteria in recent years (Carvalho, 2008; Jorge, 2010).

The regulation of the SUS came into force through the laws of 1990 # 8.080 and # 8.142, which composed the so-called 'Health Organic Law'. Both were introduced by the Executive, which could not be different, since only this branch has the constitutional competence to initiate proposals that broach on the structure of activities under their responsibilities. The matter went through the National Congress for a little over a year and was vetoed by President Collor de Mello, with 26 partial blocks, one of them excluding an article about the funding of SUS.

In the face of a lack of resources, a temporary contribution was created about financial movements, CPMF, through Constitutional Amendment 12, on 15 August 1996. Its resources would be fully allocated to health. This tribute, which should have been temporary, was maintained until 2007 through modifications promoted by eight laws, three temporary measures and three constitutional amendments (which extended its duration or changed its rate).

Regarding the CPMF, the leadership of the Executive, in its proposal and effort for its approval by the government coalition in Congress, was crucial. This behaviour was observed in both governments, Cardoso's and Silva's.

However, CPMF promoted an increase in the resources available to the Executive Branch, but without any effective concern about broadening health funding. Despite its justification as the reason for creating and keeping the tribute, the insufficiency situation was unchanged, because other sources of funding for health were decreased (Carvalho, 2008).

Other solutions for the funding problem continued to be presented by parliamentarians. We highlight PEC 169, authored by deputies who were not part of the government coalition, introduced in July 1993, which proposed the application of fixed percentages by the federal level of social contribution resources and also 10 per cent from tax revenues. For states and municipalities, the minimum would be 10 per cent of the tax revenue. Until 1999, no measures were taken to take the proposal to be voted on the floor, because the CPMF was prioritised.

Another PEC that went through simultaneously, PEC 82, proposed in April 1995 by a coalition deputy, destined to health all of the resources stemming from the contributions of employers over their income and profit. In 2000, this PEC was approved with its content completely reformulated, resulting in Constitutional Amendment 29. The acceleration at the end of the course of the amendment relied on support by the Executive Branch, under the image of the then minister of health.

Finally, more stable criteria were established for health funding. The states were to apply a minimum of 12 per cent of their income to health actions and services, and the municipalities, 15 per cent. The federal level was not contemplated with a percentage of revenue bounding, but in 2000 it should apply the amount pledged in public health actions and services in the 1999 financial year, increased by, at least, 5 per cent. From there on, the amount would be based on the amount applied in the previous year, corrected by the nominal variation in gross national product.

After Amendment 29, an increase in the participation of municipalities and states was observed, as well as a relative retraction of the federal level (Frente Parlamentar Da Saúde, 2005, 2007; Mendes & Marques, 2009).

Although the regulation of this amendment was only approved by Congress at the end of 2011, through a complementary law proposals have been presented since 2001, with the intention of inserting a minimum percentage of the revenue for application in health by the Federation; the Executive Branch, however, remained resistant.

In 2003, with the new legislature and alternation of executive power, a coalition deputy presented PLP 01/2003, with the aforementioned objective. In the Commission for Social Security and Family (CSSF), a permanent committee in the Chamber of Deputies that has regimental competence to debate health policies, according to Carvalho (2008, p. 47), the report was approved 'under great duress', for Lula da Silva's government 'bent over backwards' not to approve the project under CSSF. The matter was finally approved in this commission in August 2004. The coalition obstructed, nonetheless, the advance of the matter in other commissions, in the Chamber Plenary and also in the Federal Senate.

Therefore, the focus was diverted to another Senate proposal, PLS 121 presented in March 2007, authored by a coalition senator, which predicted a criterion considering 10 per cent of the gross current revenue of the federal level. The matter was approved by the Senate and went through to the Chamber in 2008 (under the denomination of PLP 306/2008 – the pivotal element of the halt that was broken only in 2011), where the coalition reverted the situation. The procedures in the Chamber became conflicted and, despite the proposal urgency, it remained without deliberation by the Plenary for three years. The matter only came back to deliberation by the Plenary in 2011, after great demand from society, facing a SUS health crisis.

The Executive and its coalition could not approve the creation of their proposal, a new contribution to the fund health, due to the influence of a strong rejection by public opinion, but they used their majority in both houses to approve PLP 306/08, modified in order to keep the already existing criteria for funding by the federal level, states and municipalities.

In the regulation of Amendment 29, through Complementary Law 141, of 13 January 2012, the debate about health funding went on, with new propositions meant to institute the criterion for minimal application of the gross current revenue on health by the federal level (supported by civil society), while the Executive, already under the Rousseff administration, insisted on an alternative proposal that mitigated the increase in expenditure. Finally, the Complementary Law 141, 2012, practically maintained the funding criteria that already existed.

Besides that, the health funding subject was introduced by the government coalition in Constitutional Amendment 85, approved in February 2015, which established that the federal level must apply in health, from 2016 onwards, 13.2 per cent of its net current revenue. This proportion will be progressively increased until 15 per cent of the net current revenue, from 2020 onwards. In practice, this new criterion will decrease the federal health budget (from at least R$ 8 billion in the first two years) when compared with what would have been obtained with the previous criterion (Conselho Nacional de Secretários de Saúde, 2015). Thus, SUS remains in a chronic underfunding situation, which is reflected in the quality of the services offered to the population, which generated a new demand for legislative propositions that are intended to solve the issue. For example, the Chamber of Deputies approved, in March 2016, a proposal for Constitutional Amendment PEC1/15, authored by an opposition deputy, which considerably expands the proportions of the net current income to be applied in health, amounting to 19.4 per cent in a seven-year period.

The case of the definition of legal criteria for funding health exemplifies the occurrence of several relationship patterns between the Legislative and

Executive Branches in defining the content of policies.[9] We observed leadership situations of the Legislature (during the Constitutional Assembly, the creation of the Organic Law, and the initiatives to increase SUS resources), impasses in the projects with a high distributive conflict and impact in the federal budget, and, finally cooperation (to resolve the impasses). However, the leadership of the government coalition (not just in the Executive Branch) in the definition of the fate of the proposals was clear.

Despite its more active role in pursuing a more adequate funding for SUS, the Legislature contributed equally, as a participant in government coalitions, to the stagnation of the results below the needs for resources, in general, indicating a reduced priority of both branches to the adoption of more durable and satisfactory solutions. The dependence on external stimuli to advance the health policy agenda has made the performance of the Legislature fragmented and inconsistent.

Regarding the Executive Branch of all the governments after the Constitution of 1988, a posture for a systematic resistance to proposals that resulted in more expenditure with health funding became evident.

Actors from both branches behaved strategically and similarly during the course of propositions when they pertained to the opposition or to the government. The alternation of power in the Executive from 2003 onwards allowed us to note that those parliamentarians who were against the creation of the CPMF later decided to keep it, and those who created it and extended it were the same people responsible for its extinction. The political parties did not exhibit any consistency in their ideological stance throughout this long debate, but worked as trusted mediators of the dispute between the momentary coalitions and oppositions. This partisan vagueness induced a programmatic fragmentation of the legislatures that followed the Constitutional Assembly. The case suggests that inside the government coalitions themselves there is a degree of fragmentation, since the originators of proposals, rapporteurs and presidents of commissions involved in the impasse situations, at least in the Chamber, belonged to the coalition parties.

The analysis indicates that the 'constitutionalisation' of SUS has been ruling the debate in the direction of an expansion of funding and of resisting a complete destructuration of the policy. The basic guidelines of SUS were formally maintained, even in the face of the power of government coalitions at the constitutional level, and also in the face of the resistance signalled by the Executive of several governments to expand funding for the health sector. However, the influence of the Constitution is not enough to substantiate a sufficient expansion of resources, according to its guidelines.

In any event, advances were observed in the rules produced (stemming from solutions defined by the government coalitions), though not on a level that effectively promotes the ability of citizens to obtain a proper health situation. It seems that only more autonomy of the Legislature in front of the

Executive Branch to solve properly the problems it has been exposing would be able to implement the public health policy intended by the creators of the Constitution.

This suggests that, in Brazil, the Legislature shares the power with the Executive Branch in defining policies and is not a sheer arena for debates, but has been transformative, especially in defining the larger guidelines for public policies, and, also, less efficiently, in the production and modification of rules necessary for the implementation of said policies.

Conclusion

Thus, in light of the case studies we have described, how can we classify the Brazilian Legislative Branch? In the continuum of Polsby's typology, it certainly is closer to the transformative pole than to the arena pole. Considering the classification proposed by Santos, it does not seem adequate to position it in the 'reactive' category just for the degree of predominance of initiative of the Executive Branch in the cases examined in the education sector.

The protagonism of the members of the Legislative Branch was demonstrated in all of the cases that we analysed, both in a context where the Executive Branch intended to approve policies (for the education sector) and in the context where it tried to block changes in the funding policies (for the health sector). The complications during the course of the constitutional or infraconstitutional changes have shown important proposals from the Legislature that were not present in the original proposals of the president of the Republic. Although we also observed actions that demonstrated legislative resistance, the inclusion of these novelties did not necessarily provoke a reaction to the proposals, but rather additions of relevant items for educational policies that were not originally predicted. Besides that, in much of the legislative appreciation, a collaborative articulation arose between the two branches, as exemplified by the incremental advances in health funding.

Establishing a dialogue with other studies, the conclusions we obtained: enhance the works that indicate the relevance of the actions of the Legislative Branch in the definition of public policies (Cruz, 2009; Diniz, 2005); enrich the analyses about an occasional control of the Legislative Branch by the Executive Branch (Pereira & Mueller, 2000) or the agenda power of the president of the Republic (Amorim Neto & Santos, 2003); reinforce the universalist position of the Legislative Branch in great public policy issues (Lemos, 2001); confirm the partisan discipline in plenary votes (Amorim Neto & Santos, 2003; Figueiredo & Limongi, 1996); expose the collaborative and assertive performance of the Legislative Branch with the Executive Branch, without detriment to governability (Diniz, 2005); and contradict, as pointed out by Ricci (2003), the positions that affirm that the Legislative Branch is a deterrent space for the implementation of innovative policies and that their interventions would result in proposals marked by the prevalence of particularistic interests (Ames, 2003; Mainwaring, 1999).

Thus, the observation of concrete cases of policy production goes against the theses that attribute a lesser role to the Legislature or that point out extreme difficulties for the governability in the Brazilian coalition presidentialism. The Brazilian Congress, in theses, seems to have been, at the same time, active, reactive, collaborative and innovative.

Notes

1. A synthesis of the operations of the 'system of legislative production' at the federal level of Brazil is available in Gomes (2012).
2. The cases were summarised based on the research conducted for the political science doctorate thesis of the authors. Martins (2010) approached policies in education, and Gomes (2011) studied health policies.
3. This difference in the context of education and health policies demanded that, for the latter, we look for further details in the identification of the proposals originating from the Legislative Branch, while, in the education case, this approach was unnecessary due to the predominance of the Executive Branch initiative in the analysed proposals.
4. The Proposal for a Constitutional Amendment proposed by the president of the Republic in 1995 created the Fundo de Desenvolvimento e Manutenção do Ensino Fundamental e de Valorização do Magistério (Fund for the Development and Maintenance of Elementary Education and Appreciation of Teaching) – FUNDEF. In Brazil, each federation) is legally required by the Constitution to apply a minimum percentage of its income from taxes to the upkeep and development of teaching. For states, the Federal District and towns, this percentage is 25 per cent. The Proposal for a Constitutional Amendment instituted, in each state, the fund, made up of three-fifths of this set of resources, which started to be redistributed between the state government and the townships, according to the number of enrolments in their respective networks of public basic schooling. This first redistributing mechanism was effective for 10 years. Besides that, the proposal envisaged the adoption of socio-economical priority criteria for acceptance into nursery education funded by public power and opened possibilities to eliminate or restrict the gratuity constitutional principle in public higher education. The National Congress approved the basic education fund but rejected the changes related to the other educational levels, due the interpretation that they would constitute restriction to social rights universally guaranteed by the Federal Constitution of 1988.
5. Brazilian education is organised in two levels: basic and higher education. Basic education, on the one hand, has three stages: nursery education (day-care, for babies to three-year-olds; and preschool, for four- and five-year-olds); ensino fundamental (elementary school) (with a duration of nine years, from when the children are six years old); and ensino médio (high school) (with a minimum duration of three years, in principle for 15- to 17-year-old youths). Mandatory schooling ranges from four- to 17-year-olds. Higher education offers undergraduate and graduate degrees.

79

6. While keeping the same redistributing dynamics, the second proposal broadened the reach of the fund, which started being called Fundo de Manutenção e Desenvolvimento da Educação Básica e de Valorização dos Profissionais da Educação (Fund for the Maintenance and Development of Basic Education and for the Appreciation of Education Professionals), reaching from children's education (early childhood) to high school and encompassing four-fifths of the resources the states, the Federal District and the towns should apply in the maintenance and development of education.

7. The system for evaluating higher education was initially regulated in 1995. The legislation was changed in 2004.

8. The success rate refers to the proportion of proposals that were converted into legal rules, among those presented by a certain author. The dominance rate, in turn, refers to the proportion of propositions that a certain author converted into legal rule, among those converted into legal rule in the grand author pool.

9. Similar findings with regards to the types of relationship between the Legislative and Executive were reported in a more quantitative approach of the legislative production system of Brazil (Gomes, 2012).

Disclosure statement

No potential conflict of interest was reported by the authors.

ORCiD

Fábio de Barros Correia Gomes ⓘ http://orcid.org/0000-0002-5492-9830
Ricardo Chaves de Rezende Martins ⓘ http://orcid.org/0000-0001-6368-7100

References

Abranches, S. (1988). Presidencialismo de Coalizão: O Dilema Institucional Brasileiro. *Dados - Revista de Ciências Sociais, 31*(1), 5–34.
Amaral, A. R. V. P. (2009). *O Parlamento Brasileiro - Processo, Produção e Organização Legislativa: O Papel das Comissões em Perspectiva Comparada* (Master's thesis). Instituto Universitário de Pesquisas do Rio de Janeiro / Centro de Formação da Câmara dos Deputados, Rio de Janeiro, RJ. Retrieved May 3, 2016, from http://bd.camara.gov.br/bd/bitstream/handle/bdcamara/6504/parlamento_brasileiro_amaral.pdf?sequence=4.
Ames, B. (2003). *Os Entraves da Democracia no Brasil*. Rio de Janeiro: Editora FGV.
Amorim Neto, O., & Santos, F. (2003). O Segredo Ineficiente Revisto: o que Propõem e o que Aprovam os Deputados Brasileiros? *Dados – Revista de Ciências Sociais, 46* (4), 661–698.
Baptista, T. W. F. (2003). *Políticas de Saúde no Pós-Constituinte: um Estudo da Política Implementada a partir da Produção Normativa dos Poderes Executivo e Legislativo no Brasil* (Doctoral dissertation). Instituto de Medicina Social, Universidade do Estado do Rio de Janeiro, Rio de Janeiro, RJ.
Baptista, T. W. F. (2010). Análise da Produção Legislativa em Saúde no Congresso Nacional Brasileiro (1990-2006). *Cadernos de Saúde Pública, 26*(1), 97–109.
Braga, R. J. (2011). *O Processo Decisório Legislativo na Criação e Reforma do Bacen e do CMN em 1964 e 1994: Incerteza, Cooperação e Resultados Legislativos* (Doctoral dissertation). Universidade Estadual do Rio de Janeiro, Rio de Janeiro, RJ.
Carvalho, G. (2008). Financiamento da Saúde Pública no Brasil no Pós-Constitucional de 88. *Tempus - Actas de Saúde Coletiva, 2*(1), 39–51.
Conselho Nacional de Secretários de Saúde. (2015). Implicações da Emenda Constitucional n. 86/2015 para o Processo de Financiamento do Sistema Único de Saúde. *Consensus, 15*, 36–40. Retrieved May 3, 2016, from http://www.conass.org.br/consensus/implicacoes-da-emenda-constitucional-n-862015-para-o-processo-de-financiamento-sistema-unico-de-saude/.
Cruz, M. R. (2009). *Legislativo Transformador? As Modificações do Legislativo nos Projetos de Lei do Executivo* (Master's thesis). Instituto Universitário de Pesquisas do Rio de Janeiro / Centro de Formação da Câmara dos Deputados, Rio de Janeiro, RJ. Retrieved May 3, 2016 from http://www2.camara.gov.br/responsabilidade-social/edulegislativa/educacao-legislativa-1/posgraduacao/arquivos/publicacoes/teses-minter/DissertacaoMarciaRodriguesMinterIuperj.pdf.
Diniz, S. (2005). Interações Entre os Poderes Executivo e Legislativo no Processo Decisório: Avaliando Sucesso e Fracasso Presidencial. *Dados – Revista de Ciências Sociais, 48*(1), 333–369.
Figueiredo, A., & Limongi, F. (1996). Congresso Nacional: Organização, Processo Legislativo e Produção Legal. Cadernos de Pesquisas CEBRAP, 5.

Frente parlamentar da saúde. (2005). Seminário *"Um Olhar Social sobre o Orçamento Público - Saúde, Educação e Assistência Social"* (Report). Brasília, DF: Câmara dos Deputados.

Frente parlamentar da saúde. (2007). Seminário *"Saúde e Seguridade Social"* (Report). Brasília, DF: Câmara dos Deputados.

Godoi, A. M. M. (2008). *Executivo e Legislativo na Produção Legal em Saúde, de 1988 a 2008* (Monograph). Universidade do Legislativo Brasileiro / Universidade Federal de Mato Grosso do Sul, Brasília, DF.

Gomes, F. B. C. (2011). *Interações entre o Legislativo e o Executivo Federal do Brasil na Definição de Políticas de Interesse Amplo: Uma Abordagem Sistêmica, com Aplicação na Saúde* (Doctoral dissertation). Universidade do Estado do Rio de Janeiro, Rio de Janeiro, RJ. Retrieved May 06, 2016, from http://bd.camara.gov.br/bd/bitstream/handle/bdcamara/6165/interacao_legislativo_gomes.pdf?sequence=2.

Gomes, F. B. C. (2012). Cooperation, Leadership, and Impasse Between the Legislative and Executive Branches in Lawmaking by the Brazilian National Congress. *Dados – Revista de Ciências Sociais, 55*(4), 911–950. Retrieved May 6, 2016, from http://www.scielo.br/scielo.php?script=sci_arttext&pid=S0011-52582012000400003&lng=en&nrm=iso.

Jorge, E. (2010). *SIOPS como Instrumento de Gestão.* Paper presented at the I Congresso Brasileiro de Política, Planejamento e Gestão em Saúde –ABRASCO, Salvador, BA.

Lemos, L. B. S. (2001). O Congresso Brasileiro e a Distribuição de Benefícios Sociais no Período 1988-1994: Uma Análise Distributivista. *Dados – Revista de Ciências Sociais, 44*(3), 561–605.

Mainwaring, S. P. (1999). *Rethinking Party Systems in the Third Wave of Democratization: the Case of Brazil.* Stanford: Stanford University Press.

Martins, R. C. R. (2010). *O Poder Legislativo e as Políticas Públicas Educacionais no Período 1995-2010* (Doctoral dissertation). Universidade do Estado do Rio de Janeiro, Rio de Janeiro, RJ. Retrieved from http://www.bdtd.uerj.br/tde_arquivos/43/TDE-2013-02-05T101803Z-2889/Publico/tesericardomartins.pdf.

Martins, R. C. R. (2012). *O Poder Legislativo e as Políticas Públicas Educacionais no Período 1995-2010.* Brasília, DF: Câmara dos Deputados, Edições Câmara.

Mendes, A. N., & Marques, R. M. (2009). *Crônica de Uma Crise Anunciada: o Financiamento do SUS sob a Dominância do Capital Financeiro.* Paper presented at the XII Encontro de Pesquisadores da PUCSP na área da Saúde, São Paulo.

Moisés, J. A. (2011). O desempenho do Congresso Nacional no Presidencialismo de Coalizão (1995-2006). In J. A. Moisés (Ed.), *O Papel do Congresso Nacional no Presidencialismo de Coalização* (pp. 7–29). Rio de Janeiro, RJ: Konrad-Adenauer-Stiftung.

Pereira, C., & Mueller, B. (2000). Uma Teoria da Preponderância do Poder Executivo: o Sistema de Comissões no Legislativo Brasileiro. *Revista Brasileira de Ciências Sociais, 15*(43), 45–67.

Polsby, N. W. (1975). Legislatures. In F. I. Greenstein & N. W. Polsby (Eds.), *Handbook of Political Science* (pp. 257–319). Reading, MA: Addison-Wesley.

Ricci, P. (2003). O conteúdo da Produção Legislativa Brasileira: Leis Nacionais ou Políticas Paroquiais? *Dados – Revista de Ciências Sociais, 46*(4), 699–734.

Ricci, P., & Lemos, L. (2004). Produção legislativa e preferências eleitorais na Comissão de Agricultura e Política Rural da Câmara dos Deputados. Revista Brasileira de Ciências Sociais. *São Paulo, 19*(55), 107–130.

Rodrigues, M. A., & Zauli, E. (2002). Presidente e Congresso Nacional no Processo Decisório da Política de Saúde no Brasil Democrático (1985-1998). *Dados – Revista de Ciências Sociais, 45*(3), 387–429.

Rodriguez Neto, E. (2003). *Saúde: Promessas e Limites da Constituição*. Rio de Janeiro, RJ: Editora Fiocruz.

Santos, F. (2004). A Reforma do Poder Legislativo no Brasil. *Plenarium, 1*, 26–40.

Vogel, L. H. (2010). *Negociar Direitos? Legislação Trabalhista e Reforma Neoliberal no Governo FHC (1995-2002)* (Doctoral dissertation). Universidade Estadual do Rio de Janeiro, Rio de Janeiro, RJ.

Green or grey: origin, bias and fate of environmental bills in the Brazilian National Congress

Maurício Schneider ⓘ and Ana Alice Biedzicki de Marques

ABSTRACT
The Brazilian political system orbits around a powerful Executive Branch and a budget that is not mandatory, but rather a cap on expenditures. The president and ministers decide how much to spend on governmental programmes. The Legislature is considered to be reactive to the Executive, and to play a smaller role in public policies. Such preponderance of the Executive is reflected in the National Congress voting agenda, markedly dominated by bills introduced by the president, not by congressmen. The president usually introduces *medidas provisórias* (provisional measures demanding congressional referendum within 120 days) or urgent ordinary bills, leaving little room for bills introduced by deputies and senators to be considered and voted on by committees and the houses' respective plenaries. Despite presidential preponderance upon Congress, changes in environmental laws are seen by public opinion as congressmen versus presidency conflicts. Controversial bills such as the new Forest Law enacted in 2012, and others aiming to change the Mining Code, or to curb the establishment of protected areas, are viewed as threats to the environment, or opportunities to development, depending on one's point of view. Common sense tends to consider bills proposed by the Executive as initiatives to protect the environment, while the Legislature's bias would be to lax legal restrictions on the use of natural resources, thus leaving to Congress the onus of a 'grey' or negative agenda. Here the authors examine all environmental bills introduced in the Lower House (Chamber of Deputies), their goals and main subjects, in order to compare Executive and Legislative roles and partialities in writing Brazilian environmental law.

Introduction

Brazil has a bicameral legislature, The National Congress, composed of the Chamber of Deputies and the Federal Senate. The National Congress has the prerogative of making laws and is responsible for the oversight of every accounting, financial and budgetary operation regarding the Union's moneys and properties. Both houses have congressional representatives elected every four years to form a new legislature, and stages important debates and nationwide decisions, voting on bills, constitutional amendment proposals, the Union's budget and international agreements. While the Chamber of Deputies has 513 deputies, the Federal Senate has 81 senators, and the latter is expected to be a more reflective body, like other upper legislative houses (Docherty, 2002). As a result, most of the Brazilian legislative debate takes place in the Chamber of Deputies, not only because the Lower House has more representatives, but also due to the fact that bills proposed by the Executive Branch are first voted on by the deputies, leaving to the Senate only those started by senators and the bills that have already passed the Lower House.

Bills laid before the congressional houses may be of five kinds:

- Ordinary Law Bill (*projeto de lei*) – a bill to establish, amend or revoke a law or act; introduced by the president of the Republic, a deputy or a senator; the resulting Act may be vetoed by the president (and the veto may be overruled by Congress).
- Complementary Law Bill (*projeto de lei complementar*) – a bill to regulate specific constitutional clauses, introduced by the president of the Republic, a deputy or a senator; the resulting Act may be vetoed by the president (and the veto may be overruled by Congress).
- Provisional Measure (*medida provisória*) – an urgent bill introduced by the president of the Republic, with immediate effect but demanding congressional deliberation within 120 days; the resulting Act may be vetoed by the president (and the veto may be overruled by Congress).
- Constitution Amendment Bill (*proposta de emenda à Constituição*) – a bill to amend the constitution, introduced by the president of the Republic, or one-third of deputies or senators; the Amendment cannot be vetoed by the president.
- Legislative Decree Bill (*projeto de decreto legislativo*) – a bill to approve a treaty signed by the president or to revoke executive statutory instruments or other secondary legislation; the Decree cannot be vetoed by the president.

Unlike other countries with concise constitutions and general laws, Brazil has a very extensive constitution: with 362 articles, it has been amended 91 times since 1988 (year of promulgation of the seventh Brazilian constitution). This desire to legislate about every aspect of life in society also finds expression in the large number of laws and their minutely detailed legal provisions, leaving little room for interpretation or discretionary power. Thus, passing laws may be an effective way to drive policies and to have influence on the real world. In order to maintain its primacy, the Executive Branch inflates the legislative agenda with its own bills (Abranches, 1988), controls the budget and forms coalitions within Congress to achieve a marked primacy over opposition (Moisés, 2011). Some authors state that over 80 per cent of Brazilian laws were initiated by the Executive (e.g. Limongi, 2006; Pereira & Mueller, 2000), although these statistics include budgetary bills (a presidential prerogative), and do not take into account the transformations a bill suffers while being considered by Congress (sometimes a real metamorphosis). Even provisional measures are widely changed during the legislative process (de Araújo & Silva, 2012; Silva & de Araújo, 2013).

Brazil achieved global leadership in environmental issues over the last decades due to its importance in conserving the largest tracts of tropical forests and its role in the United Nations Conferences on Sustainable Development (Ferreira et al., 2014) The country's environmental laws go back to the monarchy, and the Vargas Era (1930–45, when Getúlio Vargas modernised the country while governing for successive terms as dictator or president) was very prolific in natural resources legislation, likewise the 1960s. Over the last decades, as society and technology changed, so did the law. Common sense and media coverage echo the notion of the Legislative Branch as driven by economic rather than public interests, therefore congressmen would tend to see environmental policies as curbs to development (some authors even assert there is an anti-environmentalist block acting in Congress, e.g. Accioly & Sánchez, 2012), with only a few genuine environmentalists sitting in parliament. In 2014, for instance, the Brazilian Green Party won eight seats in the Chamber of Deputies and none in the Senate. Lawmakers laying bills to promote economic growth via intensive use of natural resources, forest conversion and less pollution control would be the expected outcome of this situation.

Criticised for a lax control over deforestation and other environmental drawbacks, the Executive is seen as responsible for large environmental impacts (chiefly due to infrastructure projects; Fearnside, 2013; Reid & de Sousa, 2005), but also as the most important conservation actor. Such a view leaves to congressional representatives the unfavourable image of nature harassers, usually associated to the farmers' associations, regardless of party (Said, 2015), even though presidents often avoid using their veto power to prevent shifting environmental legislation when economic growth is at risk.

Environmental regulations are often blamed for lost productivity, reduced profits or other economic drawbacks, whereas those who advocate stringent laws suggest they not only protect people and the environment, but also bring innovation and new investments (Brunel & Levinson, 2013; Greenstone, List, & Syverson, 2012). Both biases are legitimate in a democratic society, and this paper assesses the restrictive or permissive bias of all environmental bills laid before the Chamber of Deputies since 1971, according to their initiative (Executive, Lower or Upper House), theme and passage (enacted or not). Here we explore the drivers to initiate legislative action and analyse the factors and constraints to produce the current Brazilian environmental legislation.

Methods

Our analysis is based on the Chamber of Deputies' *Sistema de Informações Legislativas* (SILEG – an indexed database of the whole legislative process within the Lower House) to retrieve all bills dealing with environmental issues comprising 11 legislatures (1971–2014). The resulting 1717 bills were then classified according to bias (permissive, neutral, restrictive), its extent (narrow, i.e. Act amendment or new law about a narrow topic, broad, i.e. new Act or Act revocation or major Act amendment, or honorific bills), origin (Senate, Chamber of Deputies or Executive) and main theme. Bias classification considered the fact that any given proposed changes in the legislation would strengthen constraints to the use of natural resources and foster conservation (restrictive), establish less strict rules (permissive) or be neutral (e.g. honorific or commemorative bills, or redundant proposals to establish already enacted clauses).

Nature and bias of proposed bills

Among 1717 environmental bills introduced before the Chamber of Deputies between 1971 and 2014, the vast majority were ordinary law bills (1543), followed by legislative decree bills (83), constitutional amendment proposals (44), complementary law bills (28) and provisional measures (19). The seven most popular topics of these bills were, by and large: solid waste management, economic incentives for conservation, flora and forest management, pollution control, penalties for environmental damage, protected areas and energy, all of which with 100 or more bills (Figure 1).

There was a marked tendency for restrictive rather than permissive proposals in all themes but mining (80.0 per cent of all mining bills were intended to soften environmental regulations). This trend mirrors the increasing relevance of environmental issues since the 1970s in the global and national agendas, and growing concerns about pollution and deforestation within the country. Table 1 shows the vast majority of bills tend to be restrictive, except for the legislative decrees proposed by deputies (roughly three-quarters of them are permissive).

Legislative decrees are often introduced in the Lower House either by the Executive, after the signing of international agreements that must be appreciated by Congress, or by congressmen willing to overrule Executive regulations. The revocation of regulations via legislative decree is possible if the Executive has bypassed a law or exceeded its constitutional competence.

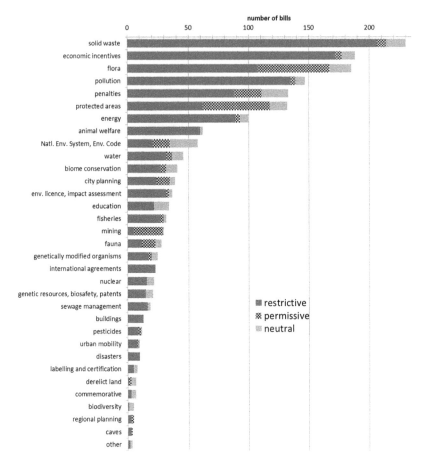

Figure 1. Environmental bills introduced in the Chamber of Deputies between 1971 and 2014.

This is seldom the case, but such bills have appeal with their constituents, despite a success rate of only 3.0 per cent. Legislative decrees are seldom enacted, but they are often introduced by deputies willing to stand ground alongside their constituents, or to react against stricter regulations from government and start negotiations.

Broad extent bills are proposed at a ratio of one-to-four relative to narrow scope proposals, and they tend to be restrictive rather than permissive (Table 2) (with the exception of legislative decree bills to revoke other regulations, as previously pointed out). Those comprehensive bills are usually aimed at unregulated or poorly regulated themes, such as animal welfare or payment for environmental services, or to provide extensive reviews of long-established acts, such as the Mining Code (enacted in 1967). When a bill does not have ample scope, it is probably an amendment proposal to

Table 1. Environmental bills introduced in the Chamber of Deputies between 1971 and 2014 according to their origin and bias.

Bill category	Origin[a]	Restrictive	Permissive	Neutral
Provisional measure	E	11 (57.9%)	5 (26.3%)	3 (15.8%)
Ordinary law	CD	1079 (69.9%)	189 (12.2%)	172 (11.1%)
	FS	42 (2.7%)	7 (0.5%)	14 (0.9%)
	E	32 (2.1%)	5 (0.3%)	4 (0.3%)
Complementary law	CD	18 (64.3%)	2 (9.1%)	5 (15.9%)
	FS	1 (6.8%)		
	E	2 (2.3%)		
Constitution amendment	CD	29 (65.9%)	4 (9.1%)	7 (15.9%)
	FS	3 (6.8%)		
	E	1 (2.3%)		
Legislative decree	CD	10 (12.5%)	33 (41.3%)	1 (1.3%)
	FS		1 (1.3%)	
	E	32 (40.0%)		3 (3.8%)

[a]CD = Chamber of Deputies; E = Executive Branch; FS = Federal Senate.
Percentages are relative to the sum of bills within each category.

modify a few clauses of an existing law, in most cases trying to enact stricter rules in order to curb any given environmental impact.

Dominant issues in enacted bills

One hundred federal environmental acts have been enacted since 1971 (the most important are listed in Table 3). Almost one-third of them are legislative decrees sanctioning international agreements (e.g. the Convention on Biological Diversity). The Executive Branch negotiates such agreements; the president signs them, but protocol demands congressional approval. Among the other 72 acts, 24 concern protected areas, flora and land titles, three of the most important constraints to forest conversion in Brazil, and particularly in the Amazon.

Table 2. Environmental bills introduced in the Chamber of Deputies between 1971 and 2014 according to their extent and bias.

Bill category	Extent	Restrictive	Permissive	Neutral
Provisional measure	Broad	3 (15.8%)		1 (5.3%)
	Narrow	8 (42.1%)	5 (26.3%)	2 (10.5%)
Ordinary law[a]	Broad	247 (16.2%)	35 (2.3%)	9 (0.6%)
	Narrow	906 (59.5%)	166 (10.9%)	160 (10.5%)
Complementary law	Broad	7 (25.0%)		4 (14.3%)
	Narrow	14 (50.0%)	2 (7.1%)	1 (3.6%)
Constitution amendment	Broad	16 (36.4%)	1 (2.3%)	1 (2.3%)
	Narrow	17 (38.6%)	3 (6.8%)	6 (13.6%)
Legislative decree	Broad	20 (24.1%)	3 (3.6%)	
	Narrow	22 (26.5%)	31 (37.3%)	7 (8.4%)

[a]Twenty-one honorific ordinary law bills (all neutral by definition) have been excluded from the table to avoid uninformative lines at each bill category.
Percentages are relative to the sum of bills within each category.

Table 3. Most important environmental bills enacted by the Brazilian National Congress; international agreements, honorific bills and law amendments are omitted (numbers after slash symbol refer to the year a bill was introduced in the Chamber of Deputies, or the year of enactment).[a]

Bill	Resulting Act	Theme	Origin	Bias
OL 813/1988	Law 8723/1993	Pollution	CD	r
OL 1924/1989	Law 7802/1989	Pesticides	E	r
OL 2116/1989	Law 7797/1989	Economic incentives	E	r
OL 5788/1990	Law 10,257/2001	City planning	FS	r
OL 203/1991	Law 12,305/2010	Solid waste	FS	r
OL 1164/1991	Law 9605/1998	Penalties	E	r
OL 2249/1991	Law 9433/1997	Water	E	r
OL 2891/1992	Law 9966/2000	Pollution	E	r
OL 2892/1992	Law 9985/2000	Protected areas	E	r
OL 3285/1992	Law 11,428/2006	Flora	CD	r
OL 3792/1993	Law 9795/1999	Education	CD	r
OL 687/1995	Law 11,959/2009	Fisheries	CD	r
OL 4649/1998	Law 10,650/2003	National Environmental System	CD	r
OL 990/1999	Law 9976/2000	Pollution	CD	r
OL 1617/1999	Law 9984/2000	Water	E	r
OL 1876/1999	Law 12,651/2012	Flora	CD	p
CL 12/2003	Complementary Law 140/2011	National Environmental System	CD	r
OL 1181/2003	Law 12,334/2010	Pollution	CD	r
OL 4776/2005	Law 11,284/2006	Flora	E	r
OL 18/2007	Law 12,187/2009	Pollution	CD	r
PM 366/2007	Law 11,516/2007	National Environmental System	E	n
PM 438/2008	Law 11,828/2008	Flora	E	r
OL 5940/2009	Law 12,351/2010	Economic incentives	E	r
PM 494/2010	Law 12,340/2010	Disasters	E	r
PM 631/2013	Law 12,983/2014	Disasters	E	r
OL 7735/2014	Law 13,123/2015	Genetic resources	E	r

[a]PM = provisional measure; OL = Ordinary law bill; CL = Complementary law bill; CD = Chamber of Deputies; E = Executive Branch; FS = Federal Senate; r = restrictive; p = permissive; n = neutral.

Fourteen out of 26 laws listed in Table 3 were proposed by the Federal Government, 10 were introduced by deputies and two by senators, almost every one of them resulting in further restrictions regarding the use of natural resources and environmental services (Figure 2).

Main subjects observed in legislative initiatives

Five environmental issues dominate legislative initiatives in the Brazilian Congress, each one of them with more than a 100 proposals in the last decades: (i) waste management; (ii) green economy and energy; (iii) vegetation remnants and protected areas; (iv) pollution; and (v) penalties.

Solid waste is one of the biggest environmental challenges currently faced by Brazil. With 84.4 per cent of the country's 191 million inhabitants living in urban areas, litter collection and disposal schemes are unevenly managed by 5565 municipal counties (IBGE, 2010, 2011). Before 2010, when Law 12,305 was enacted, there was no Federal Act ruling solid waste management. Literally dozens of bills were attached to Bill 203/1991 through the years, until

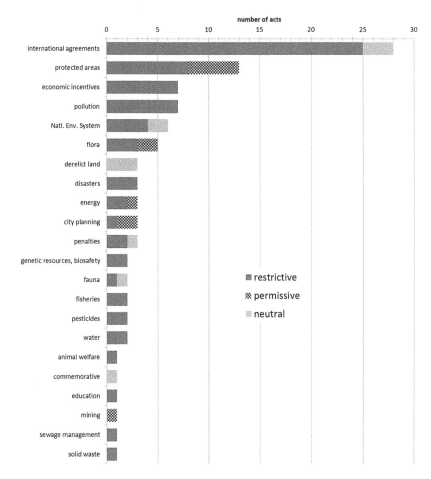

Figure 2. Number of enacted environmental laws since 1971 according to theme and bias.

they passed by both legislative houses and were sanctioned by the president. The resulting Act grouped several clauses that were previously scattered in decrees and regulations, and introduced new county management and recycling policies and product life cycle obligations to industry, commerce and customers (Juras, 2015). The claim for change in waste management policies explains why so many bills were introduced, mostly with a restrictive bias (206 out of 230).

Rewarding cooperation proved to be effective in implementing environmental policies (Shogren, 2012), and it is no surprise that economic incentives for green economy and energy summed up 285 bills, ranging from biofuels to petroleum royalties and taxation. Such bills usually aim to reduce tax on recycling, renewable energy and forest and water conservation, although such tributary reliefs often fail to prosper. The enacted ones have established grants for research and development in environmental management of the hydrocarbon industry, incentives for agroforestry and two very important funds: the National Environmental Fund and the National Climate Change Fund.

Restrictions on deforestation in Brazil began in colonial times, when the Crown prohibited forest conversion to agriculture to allow selective logging of *pau-brasil* (Brazilwood, *Caesalpinia echinata*, used for dyeing before the invention of aniline), and forest set-asides within farms were repeatedly increased at every enactment of a new law (in the years 1934, 1965, 1973, 1989, 2001 and 2006). Most of the bills about flora illustrate the tug-of-war played by farmers and environmentalists for decades. That contest always tended to the latter in the legislative arena, meanwhile deforestation would reach record levels in the Amazon; even so, the Atlantic Forest (the country's most threatened biome, running along Brazil's densely populate coastal states) achieved stricter legal protection (and field enforcement) after Bill 3285/1992 (introduced by a deputy) was enacted as Law 11,428/2006. Shortly before that, Law 11,284/2006, introduced by the Executive as Bill 4776/2005, established new rules for concessions within public forests (the Federal Government pushed to ensure its approval in only 374 days, instead of the almost 15 years of the Atlantic Forest Act).

Since the 53th Legislature (2007–11), representatives may be less prone to protect the environment. Despite introducing fewer bills, an overwhelming majority of deputies, representing both large and small landholders, imposed a major reform that included an amnesty for illegal deforestation. After years of ever more restrictive rules, Brazilian forest legislation has recently changed to accommodate the interests of farmers and expand agricultural land. This controversial bill passed the Chamber of Deputies in July 2011, after almost two years of intensive parliamentary and technical discussions, and was sent to be approved by the Senate, later enacted as Law 12,651/2012. The new Forest Law aims to settle harsh contentions between government, farmers and environmentalists, and was amended via provisional measure just three days after enactment. This was the last chapter of decades of legislative turmoil that had a marked pro-environment tendency.

Protected areas established in Brazil are ruled by Law 9985/2000, which consolidated the regulations for creating and managing 12 categories of parks and reserves under the National System of Conservation Units. There is concern in several countries about legal downsizing, downgrading and degazetting (known in the literature as PADDD) of protected areas to allow forest conversion and economic land use (World Wildlife Fund, 2015), and a number of cases are known in Brazil (de Marques & Peres, 2015), including most of the permissive bills relative to protected areas illustrated in Figure 1.

Pollution, especially in urban areas, has motivated legislators to introduce 144 bills so far, mostly to foster biofuels' production and usage, to control noise pollution (which remains unregulated in the federal sphere) or to prevent greenhouse gas emissions. They succeeded in establishing strict regulations for vehicular emissions (including the end of production of car models in nonconformity with the law), controlling industrial pollution and liquid waste, escalating biofuels to reduce sulphur emissions, and banning DDT and CFCs from the country.

In order to cluster an array of penalties already enacted in several laws, and to rule about gaps in legislation regarding the environment, the Federal Government introduced Bill 1164/1991, passed seven years later as one of Brazil's legislative landmarks, the Environmental Penalties Act (Law 9605/1998) (de Araújo, 2015). The new law boosted both law enforcement by environmental agencies, and lawmaker initiatives to review the act, resulting in 88 bills proposing more severe punishments, 23 bills to soften sanctions and 22 other we considered neutral (neither permissive nor restrictive, they appoint percentages of fines to be shared among specific public programmes, or the destination of apprehended goods).

Conclusion

Brazilian legislatures tend to have a restrictive or conservationist bias, as illustrated in this paper, meaning that lawmakers intend, most of the time, to protect the environment and human health with stricter rules. How successful they are remains a topic of debate. Despite a possible setback with the approval of the latest Forest Law, congressmen have brought to completion a comprehensive set of laws that would, if reasonably enforced, improve living conditions within the country, preserve biodiversity, halt deforestation and curb carbon emissions long before the government's international commitments.

Disclosure statement

No potential conflict of interest was reported by the authors.

ORCiD

Maurício Schneider ⓘ http://orcid.org/0000-0002-1563-6111

References

Abranches, S. (1988). Presidencialismo de coalizão: o dilema institucional brasileiro [Coalition presidentialism: The Brazilian institutional dilemma]. *Dados, 31,* 5–38.
Accioly, I., & Sánchez, C. (2012). Antiecologismo no Congresso Nacional: o meio ambiente representado na Câmara dos Deputados e no Senado Federal [Anti envir- onmentalism in the national congress: The environment represented in the chamber of deputies and the federal senate]. *Desenvolvimento e Meio Ambiente, 25,* 97–108.
de Araújo, S. M. V. G., & Silva, R. (2012). Reflexões e novas agendas de pesquisa para os estudos legislativos no Brasil [Reflections and new research agendas for legisla- tive studies in Brazil]. *Revista Ibero-Americana de Estudos Legislativos, 2,* 58–74.
de Araújo, S. M. V. G. (2015). Os fundamentos legais da Política Nacional do Meio Ambiente [The legal basis of the National Environmental Policy]. In R. S. Ganem (Org), *Legislação brasileira sobre meio ambiente: qualidade ambiental* [Brazilian legislation on the environment: Environmental quality] (pp. 39–48). Brasília: Câmara dos Deputados, Edições Câmara.
Brunel, C., & Levinson, A. (2013). Measuring environmental regulatory stringency. *OECD Trade and Environment Working Papers,* 2013/05. doi:10.1787/ 5k41t69f6f6d-en
Docherty, David C. (2002). The Canadian senate: Chamber of sober reflection or loony cousin best not talked about. *The Journal of Legislative Studies, 8,* 27–48. doi:10.1080/714003922
Fearnside, P. M. (2013). The evolving context of Brazil's environmental policies in Amazonia. *Novos Cadernos NAEA, 16,* 9–25. doi:10.5801/ncn.v16i2.1380
Ferreira, J., Aragão, L. E. O. C., Barlow, J., Barreto, P., Berenguer, E., Bustamante, M., … Zuanon, J. (2014). Brazil's environmental leadership at risk. *Science, 346,* 706– 707. doi:10.1126/science.1260194
Greenstone, M. List, J. A., & Syverson, C. (2012). *The effects of environmental regu- lation on the competitiveness of U.S. Manufacturing (NBER WP 2012-013).* Chicago: MIT.
IBGE. (2010). *Atlas do censo demográfico 2010/IBGE.* [Demographic census atlas 2010] Rio de Janeiro: Instituto Brasileiro de Geografia e Estatística.
IBGE. (2011). *Atlas de saneamento 2011.* [Sanitation atlas 2011] Brasília: Instituto Brasileiro de Geografia e Estatística.
Juras, I. A. G. M. (2015). Poluição e qualidade ambiental [Pollution and environ- mental quality]. In R. S. Ganem (Org), *Legislação brasileira sobre meio ambiente: qualidade ambiental* [Brazilian legislation on the environment: Environmental quality] (pp. 17–28). Brasília: Câmara dos Deputados, Edições Câmara.
Limongi, F. (2006). A democracia no Brasil: presidencialismo, coalizão partidária e processo decisório [Democracy in Brazil: Presidentialism, party coalition and decision-making]. *Novos Estudos-CEBRAP, 76,* 17–41.

de Marques, A. A. B., & Peres, C. A. (2015). Pervasive legal threats to protected areas in Brazil. *Oryx*, *49*, 25–29. doi:10.1017/S0030605314000726

Moisés, J. Á. (2011). O desempenho do Congresso Nacional no Presidencialismo de Coalizão (1995–2006) [The performance of the National Congress in the coalition presidentialism (1995–2006)]. In J. Á. Moisés (Org.), *O papel do Congresso Nacional no presidencialismo de coalizão* [The role of the National Congress in the coalition presidentialism] (pp. 7–29). Rio de Janeiro: Konrad-Adenauer-Stiftung.

Pereira, C., & Mueller, B. (2000). Uma teoria da preponderância do poder Executivo: O sistema de comissões no Legislativo brasileiro [One theory of the preponderance of the Executive branch: The committee system in the Brazilian legislature]. *Revista Brasileira de Ciências Sociais*, *15*, 45–67.

Reid, J., & de Sousa, W. C. (2005). Infrastructure and conservation policy in Brazil. *Conservation Biology*, *19*, 740–746. doi:10.1111/j.1523-1739.2005.00699.x

Said, F. P. (2015). *A atuação da Frente Parlamentar da Agropecuária na votação da nova lei florestal brasileira: onde está o partido político?* [The performance of the Agricultural Parliamentary Front in the vote of the new Brazilian forest law: where is the political party?] (Unpublished Bachelor's thesis). Brasília: Universidade de Brasília.

Shogren, J. (2012). Behavioural economics and environmental incentives. *OECD Environment Working Papers*, *49*, 1–32.

Silva, R. S., & de Araújo, S. M. V. G. (2013). Ainda vale a pena legislar: a atuação dos agenda holders no Congresso brasileiro [Still worth legislating: Seeking the agenda holders in congress]. *Revista de Sociologia e Política*, *21*, 19–50. doi:10.1590/S0104-44782013000400002

World Wildlife Fund. (2015). PADDDtracker: Tracking protected area downgrading, downsizing, and degazettement [Beta version]. Retrieved from www.PADDDtracker.org.

Brazilian Parliament and digital engagement

Antonio Teixeira de Barros, Cristiane Brum Bernardes and Malena Rehbein

ABSTRACT

This paper examines how new technologies are employed by the Brazilian Chamber of Deputies to stimulate experiences of digital engagement. It also evaluates how new technologies are put in practice by the institution, considering its potentialities and limitations in mediating the relationship between the parliament and the citizens. This analysis is anchored in concepts put forth by Polsby about arena parliaments and transformative parliaments, in order to evaluate which of these models of engagement tools have greater potential. The study concludes that the use of digital technologies by the Brazilian Parliament is very diverse, with a variety of tools that allow for the interaction and engagement of citizens, although these tools have the greatest potential for the arena parliament model.

Introduction

In the context of consolidation and deepening of the Brazilian democratic system, this legislature faces some specific challenges, such as greater institutional visibility, interaction with civil society, and transparency of its political actions. These three aspects are intrinsically related, since visibility entails transparency and interaction is essential for political activity carried out 'among men', as defined by Arendt (1958). It is also constructed by relationships and interactions between people, which historically led to the current model of representative democracy.

In this perspective, the role of parliament understood as a space in which social demands are externalised (Habermas, 1991) is essential for strengthening the public sphere, especially because institutional visibility, transparency and political engagement are essential elements for strengthening the public sphere and, by extension, democracy. The purpose of this work is to analyse how new technologies are employed by the Brazilian Chamber of Deputies to stimulate experiences of engagement and political participation, and to verify how to bring to fruition some aspects of the use of new technologies, their potentialities and limitations. Moreover, it also examines how these elements are institutionally articulated in order to stimulate the political action of citizens and their performance in the public sphere, in regards to the action of the legislature, in the context of strengthening of Brazilian democracy. In the final considerations, the paper draws attention to the lack of commitment to these initiatives by members of the parliament, which is seen as one of the main challenges to realising the role of increasing engagement with citizens.

We intend to evaluate how the interactive actions being currently held at the Brazilian Parliament are related to a perspective of the parliament seen as transformative or as arena type, according to Polsby's (1975) definition. An arena parliament, explains the author, is one where debate is the most important activity, with a limited role in the legislative process (exemplified in its most extreme by the United Kingdom). On the other hand, a transformative parliament would be one with an important role in all phases of the legislative process, regardless of the origin of said process (Polsby uses the United States of America as an example of this case). In an arena parliament, the power to decide seems to be outside the House, mainly in the Executive Branch, or in government, once its leaders are chosen by parliament. This type of parliament tends to endorse the choices of the Executive Branch of the government. In a transformative legislature, decisions can be taken and transformed in different spheres (committees, plenum, leadership meetings, etc.), even if a proposal comes from the Executive. Polsby also argues that arenas suffer a great impact from external forces in the form of pressure groups which support parliamentarians, while internal structures and subcultural norms are the main forces in transformative legislatures.

Cox and Morgenstern (2001) complement Polsby's statement that democracy in Latin America pertains to a third type, which they call 'reactive parliament', because the Executive has a strong power of decision in defining the agenda and creating bills sent to Congress, but the Legislative reacts to its power by debating, changing bill drafts and generally exerting a strong voice in the legislative process, although the final word can only come from the Executive through its power of veto. The notion of a reactive legislature – or levels of power in policy-making – originates from Michael Mezey's discussion about the constraints the parliament can impose on the government. According to his classification, there are three discrete categories of power: (1) strong policy-making power, if parliament can alter and reject proposals from the Executive Branch; (2) modest policy-making power, if they can modify the proposals, but not reject them; and (3) little or no policy-making power, if the Legislature can neither modify nor reject proposals from the Executive Branch (Mezey, 1979, pp. 155–156).

Instead of placing the Brazilian Congress near the extremes posed by Polsby, or other categorisations such as those proposed by Mezey or Cox and Morgenstem, we conduct an analysis of channels of engagement designed

97

by the institution based on the perspective draft by Polsby. This entails examining whether these tools are stimulating activities more related to an arena or a transformative perspective of parliaments. Before starting the analysis, however, the paper addresses in detail the activities developed to facilitate the interaction between the Chamber and external social forces.

We seek to analyse the consequences of the advent of new media on the Chamber of Deputies from the late 1990s to the early 2000s, when the information and advertising system of the organisation was remodelled. The changes include strategies for publicity and visibility of political and institutional communication, as well as tools and channels for engagement and interactivity used by the Chamber to support actions for the improvement of political democracy. The scope of this article can be expressed in the following questions. (a) What are the characteristics of the main institutional digital mechanisms of the Chamber designed to encourage democratic participation and promote digital engagement? (b) What are the functions and objectives of these tools in terms of engagement? (c) How are these tools related to the arena parliament and transforming parliament models? (d) Which results are amenable to observation so far?

To address these questions better, we start from the two main reasons pointed to by political and institutional actors in order to create channels of interactivity inside the Brazilian Parliament, which can be taken as initial assumptions and justifications for the proposed study: (1) the argument based on the constitutional principle of publicity; and (2) the need to contrast the negative agenda of the private media with respect to the Legislature, or to overcome the 'crisis of political communication' (Coleman, Taylor, & Donk, 1999) and the 'unpopularity of parliaments' (Power, 2012). Publicity regarding government actions has been duly defended by Norberto Bobbio, according to whom 'political power is public ... even when it is not public, does not act in public, is hidden from the public, is not controlled by the public' (Bobbio, 2005, p. 28). As pointed out by Norton (2007), the roles performed by representatives are good enough reason to augment the relationship between parliament and citizens, since the members of parliament act as links between society and the government and promote a direct defence of the interests of the citizens. To enforce the constitutional principle of publicising public acts, parliaments around the world have developed a number of visibility strategies, which have resulted in public information systems and transparency, such as the one created by the Brazilian Chamber of Deputies.

As some authors emphasise, political trust is not exclusively linked to rational judgement, but also relies on symbolic representations produced with irrational and affective responses originating from the citizens in relation to political institutions (Bernardes & Leston-Bandeira, 2016; Leston-Bandeira, 2012a; Pitkin, 1967). In this way, just to offer information to people is not enough from a public system of political interaction. The system needs to promote engagement and implement tools of democratic participation of recipients and users of these information services. It is no coincidence that these goals – to widen public understanding of parliament and to stimulate the participation of citizens in the legislative process – were stressed in the World E-Parliament Report (2012) as main objectives of legislatures around the world.

Many studies conducted since the 1990s highlight the potential of information and communication technologies (ICTs) as tools for social engagement (Carman, 2009; Coleman et al., 1999; Dai, 2007; Lilleker & Jackson, 2009) and, as consequence, as a way to mitigate the issue of low trust and negative image of legislative institutions (Leston-Bandeira, 2012a; Walker, 2012). However, it is important to remember Norris (2001) and others when they point out that: (1) the use of ICTs by institutions is traditional and not as innovative as it could be; and (2) the internet reinforces activism from people who have already been participating in politics, a point confirmed by posterior analysis (Dai & Norton, 2007; Gibson, Lusoli, & Ward, 2008).

The study is structured in two parts. The first comprises a mapping of the recent experience of the Chamber, with an inventory and an explanation of digital channels of engagement. The second part presents an analysis of the initial results and the progress of these mechanisms associated with a discussion about issues such as the effectiveness of these engagement tools to inform citizens and to enable their political interactions, coupled with a debate about transparency and engagement, specifically related to the Brazilian experience in this field.

Digital engagement tools of the Chamber of Deputies

The digital engagement tools currently used by the Chamber cover interaction channels managed by the administrative offices of the institution and mechanisms of engagement offered by institutional media. In the first category, we can mention institutional email form (Contact Us), public hearings, social media accounts of the institution and the e-Democracy platform.[1] In its own right, the institutional communication service, which includes institutional media (TV, radio and online news agency), comprises a lot of digital channels of interaction with the public, such as profiles in social media platforms (Twitter and Facebook, for example), electronic surveys, email and chats. Many of these institutional mechanisms are geared towards output in the legislative process, while some channels of communication of the legislative media, such as their profiles in social media platforms, for example, can offer external support for the debates or give them more visibility in the public sphere, but are not designed to interfere directly in the production of laws.

The institutional policy of encouraging engagement and political participation was reinforced by the Chamber of Deputies in April 2011, when a
working group was created to systematise tools of engagement and popular
participation in the House and to facilitate the filing of bills by members of
the general society. The working group is composed of parliamentarians
and civil officers and is responsible for evaluating the many channels, such
as 0800 or Dial-to-the-House (toll free[2]) and e-Democracy,[3] and for
seeking solutions to promote integration between the channels of the legislative and administrative spheres. This distinction is very complex, since, in
theory, all the activities of the Legislature are related to their core business.
Briefly, the legislative sphere would be more related to the work of parliamentarians' offices, committees, the chair of the House and other bodies directly
linked to parliamentary action and legislative processes. The administrative
sphere, in general, includes offices focused on institutional policy, relationships with other institutions of the state and society, such as the media and
its interaction channels, the General Office (responsible for all payments of
the Chamber), library, and other sections responsible for internal administration and tasks related to the maintenance of the institution itself.

From this perspective, the channels of the legislative sphere are those that
allow a more direct engagement in the process of production of laws and legislative decisions, while other engagement tools target administrative bodies
of the House and are meant to contribute to the functioning of these different
areas. Internally, this division between legislative and administrative does not
appear to be irrelevant and, in practice, it has direct implications in the formulation of policies for participation and engagement, in managing and
defining strategies for interaction of channels, in the relationship with parliamentary offices and in the power relationships between administrative bodies
of the upper hierarchy of the bureaucratic structure. However, we do not
intend to analyse the details of this process, but rather outline the landscape
that serves as a contextual environment for the debate on interactivity and
engagement within the proposal of taking stock of the recent performance
of the Brazilian Chamber of Deputies.

We explore the Brazilian Parliament's tools for engagement in the next
section.

Legislative channels of engagement and interactivity

Public digital hearings

The use of public hearings as a tool of engagement has increased since the end
of the 1990s, after deputies realised they attract media coverage and, consequently, can act as a springboard for their political aspirations. Before the
internet, hearings would be transmitted by radio or television. Since
October 2009, the Brazilian population can also watch selected meetings

through the parliament website (the service must be requested by parliamentarians), and can also contribute to the debate in real time through the e-Democracy platform. In 20009, WebCâmara (WebChamber), a broadcasting service designed to show what is happening in committee meetings, was created.

Thus, public digital hearings sponsored by the standing committees of the Chamber of Deputies are geared towards the discussion of public policy and issues of social interest and can also be included in the list of tools of engagement, as part of the vector Society ⇒ Institution. These public debate sessions are conducted with the purpose of allowing representatives of organisations and social movements, as well as scientists, experts and community leaders, to express themselves. They are officially invited to present evidence on several issues, in order to offer support to the work of parliamentarians in their activities as committee chairmen, rapporteurs and authors of bills.

Since most sessions occur from Tuesday to Thursday, the period in which lawmakers focus their activities in Brasilia, many events end up happening at the same time, in committee plenaries, which makes it impossible to have full coverage by the House media. WebCâmara was a solution to try and raise the visibility of hearings and meetings that cannot be attended by people who live far from Brasília. Thus, the user interested in the subject of a hearing may watch it in real time, even if it is not being transmitted by the TV or radio services of the House.[4]

These hearings are considered essential to strengthening the practices of democracy and citizenship in the current context. Unlike a public session in which the audience only watches the debate, representatives of the community may manifest actively in a public hearing, also questioning parliamentarians and other participants, assuring citizens the right to participate and to be heard. Thus, this instrument allows for the strengthening of the relationship between society and state, as well as enabling the renewal of dialogue between public agents and the population. It is also considered a 'suitable mechanism for consensus-building in public opinion', and an 'element of power democratization and way of participation in public power' (Dal Bosco, 2003, p. 735), exactly because the main function of the public hearings is to provide information to parliamentarians, which implies the presentation of a variety of perspectives and approaches, as points of views and interests defended by the segments consulted (Santos & Almeida, 2005).

In 2014 there were 734 public hearings, each one with an average of four people invited from civil society, which means 2936 representatives of the various segments and social categories in a year. The guests from civil society are relevant from the perspective of the informational role of public hearings. A greater variety of guests also means greater diversity of perspectives and opinions, after all.

E-Democracy

The e-Democracy platform was established in 2009 with the objective of becoming a social networking platform of sorts - with virtual communities - to encourage engagement and popular participation in the formulation and discussion of legislative proposals and to divulge the progress of matters under discussion. The tool allows people to make suggestions to legislative proposals in progress, to prepare drafts of bills collaboratively and to share information that will contribute to discussions. This new tool was created in order to meet the principles of participatory democracy, as envisaged in the constitution of 1988, when mentioning referendums, plebiscites and popular participation in the formulation of legislative proposals.

By July 2015 there were over 34,383 citizens enrolled in virtual communities of e-Democracy.[5] The platform has already garnered more than 36 million views since 2011 (data collected in July 2015). In order to contextualise these data, it is appropriate to recall that the total population of Brazil is approximately of 200 million people and, of this total, approximately 50 per cent are also internet users as shown in Table 1.

In August 2010, e-Democracy was selected as among the 20 best democracy experiments in the world by the *Vitalising Democracy through Participation* programme of the German Bertelsmann Stiftung Foundation. There were 158 projects taking place in 36 countries. According to Faria (2012), institutional e-Democracy projects, i.e. those developed by the state, have the advantage of enabling participation in the internal processes of each public organisation. The author believes that, therefore, their existence 'allows effective impact on decision making, but also presents a number of limitations, especially regarding the accessibility of people to these channels, and other problems expressed in the development of such practices' (Faria, 2012, p. 246).

One of the difficulties faced in the process of deployment of the tool at the Chamber of Deputies was 'a growing tension between the new logic of flow of information and social interaction with the solidity of public institutions based on Weber's model of hierarchical and procedural administrative organization' (Faria, 2012, p. 248). According to the author, the various areas of the Chamber needed to adapt to new demands generated by e-Democracy - for instance, the larger flux of information created with comments and suggestions made by citizens challenges the ability of a small team to organise such an amount of data - which resulted in resistance between the civil officers themselves.

Table 1. Topics/draft bills with most participation in e-Democracy.

E-Democracy	Comments	New suggestions	Page views	Status
Civil Procedure Code	142	283	76,442	Draft Bill in the House Floor
Internet Civil Landmark	139	100	141,215	Draft Bill in the House Floor
Commercial Code	24	22	31,123	Draft Bill in the Committees
Statute of Disabled People	192	518	24,256	Draft Bill in the Committees

There are other challenges to the institution, especially the ambiguity behind these mechanisms, which can facilitate and stimulate digital engagement for citizens and can also create obstacles to it. One of these challenges is regarding the citizens, institutions and politicians learning how to use these tools. All people involved should be able to understand the functioning of the digital tools and to create information through digital tools, which means they have to be literate in digital language. Another difficulty could be the fact that data generated by this use, as we mentioned earlier, should be organised and managed to produce useful political information to all political actors involved in the process.

At the moment, these issues are being addressed by the Chamber's team, along the process of increasing digitalisation and transparency. But issues such as the organisation and management of data or the need for digital literacy of users have not been properly resolved yet.[6]

Parliamentary website

The parliamentary website (www.camara.leg.br) has existed since 2000 and its content is managed by a committee of experts and technicians from different areas of information of the House. It is important to emphasise, at this point, that members of parliament do not participate in the process of managing the website. Unfortunately, data on digital tools of engagement have not yet been systematised, but some studies are starting to analyse the use of these channels by the Chamber. Barros, Bernardes, and Dias (2009), Marques (2011) and Miola (2011) highlight several tools of engagement and political participation present in the Chamber website, such as emails and forms, chats, polls, comments on news and public forums, also analysing its effects. Marques mentions that in 2006, for example, the Contact Us service received over 92,000 posts (Marques, 2011, p. 105). Given this number and to streamline the response process, the Contact Us forwards messages to different sectors, which provide the answers directly to users.

The Online Portal of the Chamber of Deputies (www.camara.leg.br) was considered to be the one with the highest degree of interactivity with the public among the parliaments of South America (Braga, 2008). A more recent study has mapped both the accesses and profile of citizens who use the content of the website and, specifically, the E-Democracy platform (Stabile, 2012). Some of its results are commented on in the next item of this paper, but it seems worth noting that 80 per cent of users are looking for information about parliament's agenda and the stage of bills in the legislative process (Stabile, 2012, p. 77).

Within the website, we should highlight the Chamber Online News Agency, which offers several channels to promote the engagement and participation of society. Among the digital tools are those described in Table 2.

Table 2. Descriptions and results of use of the main tools.

Tool	Description	Results from 2005 to July 2015
Contact us	A contact from the public through the official email	14,703 emails in the period
Polls	Poll surveys on topics defined by the Communication Office, conducted through adhesion of people who call to the Chamber toll-free number	5604 polls were done, with a total of 15,280,203 votes in the period
Chat	Chat with MPs with citizens' participation	79 were held during the period
Comments on news	Comments made on any news of the agency	4987 was the monthly average in the period
Talk to the MP	A link where the citizens can send their question directly to the MP they want to reach	75 opinions is the daily average during the period
Interactive public hearings	Citizens can pose questions through an online chat moderated by a civil officer who will select the best ones to be answered by the official participants	737 interactive events in the period

Source: Prepared by the authors.

Periodically, data collected in polls and chats are sent to committees that are discussing the related issues. The purpose of these reports is to provide information to parliamentarians about the citizen manifestations through the channels of interactivity. Information collected through these tools is systematised and organised to show what some of the opinions expressed by the population about and to their representatives are, with the purpose of fostering an interface between parliament and society.

According to Table 2, from 2005 to July 2015, 5604 polls were done, with a total of 15,280,203 votes. Controversial issues gather significant participation, such as the bill that created the Family Code, which reached more than 10 million votes[7] in 2014. Same-sex union, which is among the polls that have already closed, reached 19,268 votes; the affirmative actions to get into a federal university reached 12,850 votes. The number of chats – which are usually held with rapporteurs of important bills – was 79 until the same date. The monthly average of news comments is 4987, and the number of opinions sent to the deputies cited is 75 per day.

These data show that part of the Brazilian population is interested enough in the legislative agenda to make collaborations through the website, and that there are issues – especially those that result in large controversies – that can mobilise the engagement of a larger number of citizens.

TV Câmara

It is worth mentioning that the Brazilian Chamber of Deputies maintains a TV channel as part of its communication system. The purpose of TV Câmara is to transmit legislative sessions and disseminate information on parliamentary activities without the mediation of private television channels. The TV channel maintains a Contact Us service, as well as email addresses to specific interactive shows and for agenda suggestions. There are specific

Table 3. Messages sent to the Chamber TV.

Types of message sent to the Chamber TV	Participations	%
Compliments	323	1.17
Free comments	214	0.78
Complaints	367	1. 33
Requests	3436	12.47
Suggestions	432	1.57
Participation in a programme through Dial-to-the-Chamber	22,782	82.68
Total:	*27,554*	*100.00*

Source: TV Câmara.
Note: The participation through Dial-to-the-Chamber could happen by telephone or online in this case.

blogs for some TV shows, such as *House On*, a game show targeted at young people. Table 3 summarises the messages sent to the TV and its various shows through the channels available (Contact Us and emails) in 2014.

Through Dial-to-the-Chamber, the TV itself received 10,190 messages throughout the period. That means messages sent by viewers to deputies who participate in parliamentary debates and live interviews, or messages to the journalists who have produced these debates and TV shows (criticism, suggestions, questions, etc.). This shows that the TV channel itself works as a mechanism for stimulating the engagement of citizens, who give opinions during the debate and interview programmes with parliamentarians. Of course, parliamentary opinion, in this case, is the main stimulus for public interaction with TV Câmara, which can mean parliamentary support, complaints, and criticism as well.

Social media

The Online News Agency, the TV channel, radio and newspaper, as well as e-Democracy, Plenarinho (special page for children with legislative information) and programmes of TV Câmara all have Twitter accounts. Besides this, many of them also have profiles on Facebook, as shown in Table 4,

Table 4. Social media (2015).

Participation channel	Twitter followers	Facebook friends
Press Department	26,764	82,000
Chamber of Deputies	356,000	41,000
Online News Agency	62,862	35,286
TV	74,900	17,000
Newspaper	5751	13,849
e-Democracy	4063	9783
Radio	38,600	2230
Plenarinho	2011	3445
Total:	*570,951*	*204,593*

Source: Prepared by the authors.
Note: Despite its not belonging to the Communication Office, e-Democracy is included because it reports to the same management team of some of the tools (such as the interactive public hearings) with the Communication sector.

with data computed until July 2015. Twitter is the winner of social media, having reached 186,519 followers to that date.

Once again the data reinforce the diversity of digital tools for engagement offered by the Chamber of Deputies. There are citizens interested in interacting with the Brazilian Parliament for various technological platforms, including social media and telephone, and the point here seems to be to offer as many possibilities as possible to facilitate this contact and interaction.

Analysis of engagement mechanisms maintained by the Chamber of Deputies

According to the data presented above, it is possible to see that there are many possibilities for social engagement and political interaction that are currently offered by the Brazilian Chamber of Deputies. However, apart from the use of email, the other tools for digital participation are relatively recent; therefore the House has not yet collected, as noted, systematic data that would allow for a more insightful comparison and analysis.

In line with the purpose of this paper, we analysed the information from a qualitative perspective based on the Polsby classification (Table 5), briefly explained in the Introduction. The main point here is: are these channels for engagement more related to an arena type of parliament or to a transformative parliament?

Before the analysis, it is essential to explain the categories used in Table 5. This paper adopts a perspective of engagement as a process, similar to that used by Leston-Bandeira (2012b) when examining the case of the European Parliament. As a process, the engagement displays different steps, from information to intervention, also encompassing understanding, identification and participation as intermediate stages (Leston-Bandeira, 2012b, pp. 4–5). Citizens should start obtaining information to develop a gradual understanding of and identification with parliament, which could lead them to participate and, finally, intervene in the decision process.

The categories presented in Table 5 combine these two theoretical perspectives with the considerations of Polsby. The two first steps indicated by Leston-Bandeira – information and understanding – could be combined in what Karlsson (2013) calls accountability, since information and apprehension of the information are necessary to the social control of representatives. Identification is difficult to measure from an institutional point of view, which means that some kind of inquiry, as posed by Karlsson, would be needed to confirm whether citizens are seeing the perceiving of parliament in their lives. Thus, if Leston-Bandeira characterises the identification from the public point of view, Karlsson takes an opposing path, focusing on the institutional perspective of the process, something we also consider of interest in this paper.

Table 5. Mapping of engagement tools.

Tools	Mechanism	Main objective	Potential level of engagement related to arena parliament	Potential level of engagement related to transformative parliament	Examples
Public digital hearings	Committees considering draft bills receive written and verbal evidence, information and questions from the public through the internet while the meeting is being held	- Collect information and citizens' opinions for parliamentarians - Create a thermometer of the sorts of feelings of society - Listen to social segments and social movements - Disseminate information about the legislative process to citizens - Discuss specific topics	- Accountability/information/understanding - Inquiry/identification	- Connectivity/participation/intervention (influence on legislative decisions)	Hearing about 'Gay Cure' Hearing about Uber's regulation in Brazil
E-Democracy	A small number of bills or issues from some selected committees are chosen to be the subject of a cyber community. Online comments from citizens about the content of bills before consideration by the parliamentary committees	- Identify groups of interest related to the legislative bills or issues under discussion - Allow interaction between citizens and representatives - Provide thematic reports to the committees and the rapporteurs of the proposals - Promote collaboration between citizens, experts and representatives during production of laws	- Accountability/information/understanding - Inquiry/identification	- Connectivity/participation/intervention (influence on legislative decisions; cooperation with legislative production; suggestion of bills)	Civil Process Bill Political reform debate on the work group created for the purpose

(*Continued*)

Table 5. Continued.

Tools	Mechanism	Main objective	Potential level of engagement related to arena parliament	Potential level of engagement related to transformative parliament	Examples
Parliamentary website	A series of digital tools are available to citizens to contact the institution and obtain information about the legislative process, or to present opinions on polls or a bill's draft	- Provide information to society about legislative activities - Allow contact and interaction with the institution and representatives - Enable the expression of views about the proposals and activities of the institution - Present the opinion of society (or of segmented groups) through polls and comments	- Accountability/information/understanding - Inquiry/identification	- Connectivity/participation/intervention (suggestion of bills)	- Family Statute Disarming Statute
Chamber TV	Channel maintained by the Chamber with the objective of broadcasting meetings and parliamentary sessions, as well as debates, news and interviews with parliamentarians	- Provide information to society about the activities of the legislative organ - Ensure to parliamentarians the expression of ideas, proposals and opinions (debates and interviews) - Allow for contact and interaction with TV content managers - Enable the expression of opinions about the offered content	- Accountability/information/understanding - Inquiry/Identification		- Câmara Ligada's blog TV programme with popular participation
Social media	16 profiles are available on social media to make contact with citizens, explore their opinions, and disseminate information	- Disseminate information about institutional activities - Allow for the expression of opinions on the legislative agenda - Stimulate debate about issues and bills under discussion at the Chamber - Strengthen the contact and interaction between the Chamber and society	- Accountability/information/understanding - Inquiry/Identification		Profiles on Facebook and Twitter (official Chamber profile, Chamber TV profile, etc.

Source: Prepared by the authors.

Finally, the connectivity designed by Karlsson implies the continuity of dialogue and negotiation between representatives/represented after the elections, something that could be achieved through participation and intervention of citizens in the legislative process, as stated by Leston-Bandeira. In the empirical analysis, we have identified three different kinds of activities that could be included in this category, and comprise distinct options citizens have about participating and intervening in the legislative process. They are: influence on legislative decision, usually through pressure and opinion; cooperation in legislative production, participating in the writing of bills and amendments with representatives; and, lastly, suggestion of bills.

As a result, we have three hybrid categories to describe the levels observed in the channels of engagement designed by the Brazilian Chamber of Deputies: (1) accountability/information/understanding; (2) inquiry/identification; and (3) connectivity/participation/intervention. As pointed out, the first and the second are linked to activities that would fit properly in an arena type of parliament, while the third one is related to a transformative parliament.

After explaining the categories we are using, it is worth noticing that Table 5 provides some interesting pieces of information. First of all, it is important to highlight that different levels of engagement could be reached by each of the tools designed by the Brazilian Chamber. Most of the initiatives are focused on providing information to the population, more than establishing real forms of feedback to the institution. Nonetheless, the potential to achieve a more sophisticated level of engagement, by using tools such as digital forums for connectivity or influence in the outputs of legislative process, is related to some of them.

At its majority, the tools implemented by the Brazilian Chamber were designed to promote debate and dissemination of information and opinion between citizens and parliament. The categories of (1) accountability/information/understanding and (2) inquiry/identification are grouped in an arena perspective, since they can contribute to the process of circulation of social opinion and debate. These categories could be summarised as ways to: (1) inform society and representatives about political issues and the legislative process; and (2) help them to form opinions, serving as a basis for political action.

On the other hand, the levels of engagement related to a transformative perspective of the parliament are less common in the activities performed by the Brazilian Chamber. They are part of the decision process, and can be summarised in three different types of activity, as mentioned previously: (1) influence on legislative decision; (2) cooperation in legislative production; and (3) suggestion of bills/laws. All these activities can be performed not only by experts, which is usual in parliaments, but also by common citizens through the digital sphere. All three of them are included in our third category: connectivity/participation/intervention. These three latter categories present a potential for the level of engagement of a transformative parliament.

It is worth noticing that the e-Democracy platform can combine all these three levels, being the most sophisticated tool for engagement available in the Brazilian Parliament at the moment. In fact, through Wikilegis – a collaborative tool for elaboration and revision of bills – and its debate communities, e-Democracy combines information, collection of citizens' opinions and public influence on the result of legislative production, as shown by the examples of the Civil Process Bill and the debate about political reform. These are cases where the final versions of bills produced by the Chamber were collectively created by representatives with the help of experts and citizens.

Another important observation should be made about the word 'potential', used regarding the levels of engagement. As with all discussions regarding the internet and general digital activities, the tools examined in this paper show a great potential for stimulating and promoting political engagement by citizens. The reality of the political game, however, does not always correspond to the theoretical possibilities sought by the institutions. Because of the real circumstances of political action, one can see there are few examples of these activities. In other words, despite the potential the tools have, political actors are reluctant to implement a more sophisticated level of engagement. Many representatives, for instance, do not use these tools to improve their work or, at least, to obtain more information about public opinion. Few of them really concern themselves with how these channels might improve the quality of the legislative process and, consequently, the quality of representative democracy in Brazil.

This difficulty is related to the fact that all activities examined in this paper were designed by civil officers and implemented by them. As mentioned by Leston-Bandeira (2012b, p. 2), the highest level of autonomy and the highest investment on areas of public engagement, such as web communication offices, is one of the factors that lead to the development of digital tools. Of course its implementation had the express authorisation of the political actors – in this case, the representatives. But the initiative for their creation came from the bureaucracy, which could be another reason for the resistance to their use by the members of the parliament. The point here is that many political actors do not see the utility of these activities for their political action. Some of them just do not realise the potential of channels of engagement, but others really fear the proximity to citizens that the tools can promote, since the content and management of these channels are challenging for them in terms of the lack of control of political discourse disseminated through them and the high expenditure of resources – physical or human – in their management.

Conclusions

The data we explored show that the primary focus of the institution has been offering digital channels to receive manifestations from society, but this alone does not ensure citizen participation in the decision-making processes. There are, thus, no mechanisms to bring participation into the offices of parliamentarians, and to guarantee responses to society. To achieve that, it would still be necessary to increase awareness of policy-makers about the importance of these interactive tools for social participation.

Considering Polsby's concepts about parliament types, our findings do not allow us to say that they increase or reinforce the debate between society and parliamentarians, contributing to an arena profile, since the representatives practically do not interact with citizens. We assume, however, that the increase of information availability increases the chances of an arena situation. On the other hand, since the Legislature does not use this information for legislation, it also does not contribute to a transformative profile.

Of course, we cannot disregard the potential for both. If we follow Polsby's perspective of an arena legislature as one that suffers a great impact of external forces and promotes debate throughout the whole of society, activities that promote interaction and communication with social groups and citizens are completely justified. On the other hand, the use that parliamentarians make of these inputs could influence and change public policies, which are the legislative outcomes per se. Thus, the contribution of society can lead parliament in a direction of being more transformative or reactive (using Cox and Morgenstern concepts).

One challenge is that not all legislators are willing to negotiate their manner of using their term and to establish relationships with their constituencies. They also show difficulties in accepting or joining a system for engagement and participation that reflects the interests of the institution – after a circular relationship with the participation of society – and not necessarily involving parliamentarians. The Brazilian parliamentary culture is not always anchored on the principles of participatory and social engagement, although some traditional tolls, such as plebiscites, referendums and popular initiatives, are accounted for in the constitution of 1988. This view of Brazilian parliamentary culture is supported by the Chamber of Deputies and by representatives of civil society, but does not always resonate in the thought and conduct of deputies and their advisors, who are responsible for decisions at the administrative level.

Despite a renewal of the parliamentary culture in the past few decades, there are still members who exercise their terms based on the pillars of traditional politics, with emphasis on values of localism, authoritarianism and personalism. There are also those who rely on more formalistic concepts of representation as delegation, not as an ongoing process of relationship/ debate with society. In addition, there is the counterpoint of the political culture of the electors, who still choose representatives that display this type of parliamentary behaviour and expect old-fashioned politics. The effectiveness of a social and political engagement/participation project depends not just on the decisions of the Chamber regarding the provision and management of channels of interactivity. If parliamentarians and electors do not adhere to the institutional project of the House, the results will be restricted to the microphysics of the managerial and clerical spaces of the House, without any consequences in terms of engagement.

Notes

1. E-Democracy is a portal website created in 2009, a digital participation platform that seeks to facilitate virtual discussion between citizens and parliamentarians throughout the legislative process. It has over 34,000 registered members and 3000 discussion topics have been created. For more information, see the article by Farias and Rodrigues in this journal.
2. Because this paper comprises only digital tools, the Dial-to-the-House service – a telephone service – will not be analysed, despite being an important channel of engagement for the Brazilian strata of population that have no access to the internet and computers.
3. Since November 2013, a Hacker Laboratory has been operating inside the Brazilian Chamber of Deputies. As the initiative is still in its first steps, we do not have enough data about it to present in this study.
4. The Chamber has four legislative media: TV, radio, newspaper and news agency.
5. Citizens may register in more than one community on e-Democracy.
6. For more information on e-Democracy, see the article by Farias and Rodrigues in this journal.
7. The Family Code was a bill that, in brief, ignored any configuration of family not composed of a heterosexual couple and their children.

Disclosure statement

No potential conflict of interest was reported by the authors.

References

Arendt, H. (1958). *The human condition*. Chicago: University of Chicago Press.

Barros, A. T., Bernardes, C. B., & Dias, M. C. (2009). Perspectiva sociopolítica da interatividade nas mídias legislativas: o caso da Câmara dos Deputados. *Cadernos da Escola do Legislativo, 11*, 59–83.

Bernardes, C. B., & Leston-Bandeira, C. (2016). Information vs Engagement in parliamentary websites – a case study of Brazil and UK. Submitted for publication in: Revista de Sociologia e Política, Curitiba/PR.

Bobbio, N. (2005). *Estado, governo, sociedade. Para uma teoria geral da política*. Rio de Janeiro: Paz e Terra.

Braga, S. (2008). *Podem as TICs auxiliar na institucionalização das Democracias? Um estudo sobre a informatização dos órgãos legislativos na América do Sul e no Brasil*. Brasília: Plenarium.

Carman, C. (2009). Engaging the public in the Scottish parliament's petitions process. Edinburgh, Ipsos/Mori, undertaken on behalf of the Scottish Parliament's Public Petitions Committee. Retrieved from http://archive.scottish.parliament.uk/s3/committees/petitions/inquiries/petitionsProcess/Engagingthepublicinthepetitionsprocess.pdf.pdf on 2013/10/27

Coleman, S., Taylor, J., & Donk, W. V. (Ed.) (1999). *Parliament in the age of internet*. Oxford: Oxford University Press.

Cox, G. W., & Morgenstern, S. (2001). Comparative politics, v.33, n.2 p. 171–189. Retrieved from http://isites.harvard.edu/fs/docs/icb.topic925740.files/Week%208/Cox_Latin.pdf

Dai, X. (2007). Prospects and concerns of e-Democracy at European Parliament. *Journal of Legislative Studies, 13*(3), 370–387.

Dai, X., & Norton, P. (2007). The internet and parliamentary democracy in Europe. *Journal of Legislative Studies, 13*(3), 342–353.

Dal Bosco, M. G. (2003). Audiência pública como direito de participação. *Revista dos Tribunais. Brasília, 92*(809), 727–739.

Faria, C. F. (2012). *O parlamento aberto na era da internet*. Brasília: Edições Câmara.

Gibson, R., Lusoli, W., & Ward, S. (2008). The Australian public and politics on-line: Reinforcing or reinventing representation? *Australian Journal of Political Science, 43*(1), 111–131.

Habermas, J. (1991). *The structural transformation of the public sphere: An inquiry into a category of bourgeois society*. Boston: MIT press.

Karlsson, M. (2013). Representation as interactive communication. *Information, Communication and Society, 16*(8), 1201–1222.

Leston-Bandeira, C. (2012a). Parliaments' endless pursuit of trust: Re-focusing on symbolic representation. *The Journal of Legislative Studies, 18*(3–4), 514–526.

Leston-Bandeira, C. (2012b). The pursuit of legitimacy as a key driver for public engagement. *Parliamentary Affairs, 67*(2), 415–436.

Lilleker, D. G.; Jackson, N. A. (2009). Interacting and representing: Can Web 2.0 enhance the roles of an MP? Paper presented in ESRC Workshop, p.1–26.

Marques, J. A. (2011). Participação, instituições políticas e internet: um exame dos canais participativos presentes nos portais da Câmara e da Presidência da República. In R. Maia et al. A. Internet e participação política no Brasil (pp. 95–121). Porto Alegre: Sulina.

Mezey, M. L. (1979). Comparative legislatures. Durhan: Duke University Press.

Miola, E. (2011). Iniciativas institucionais de deliberação online: um estudo do fórum de discussão do portal da Câmara dos Deputados. In: R. C. M. Maia, W. Gomes, & F. P. J. A. Marques (Orgs.), Internet e participação política no Brasil (pp. 147–174). Porto Alegre: Sulina.

Norris, P. (2001). The digital divide. Cambridge, Cambridge University Press.

Norton, P. (2007). Four models of political representation: British MPs and the use of ICT. Journal of Legislative Studies, 13(3), 354–369.

Pitkin, H. F. (1967). The concept of representation. Berkeley: University of California.

Polsby, N. W. (1975). Legislatures. In Fred I. Greenstein e Nelson W. Polsby (Orgs.), Handbook of Political Science (pp. 257–317). Reading, MA: Addison-Wesley.

Power, G. (2012). Global parliamentary report: The changing nature of parliamentary representation. Inter-Parliamentary Union. Retrieved from http://www.ipu.org/pdf/publications/gpr2012-full-e.pdf

Santos, F., & Almeida, A. (2005). Teoria informacional e a seleção de relatores na Câmara dos Deputados. Dados, 48(4), 693–735.

Stabile, M. (2012). Democracia Eletrônica para quem? Quem são, o que querem e como os cidadãos avaliam o portal da Câmara dos Deputados. Dissertation (Master in Political Science). Instituto de Ciência Política, Universidade de Brasília.

Walker, A. (2012). A people's parliament? Parliamentary Affairs, 65, 270–280.

Open parliament policy applied to the Brazilian Chamber of Deputies

Cristiano Faria and Malena Rehbein

ABSTRACT

This article will analyse the implementation of an open parliament policy that is taking place at the Chamber of Deputies, in accordance with the guidelines of the Open Government Partnership international programme (OGP), regarding the action plan of the Opening Parliament Work Group in particular, one of the subgroups of OGP. The authors will evaluate two blocks of initiatives for open parliaments executed by the Chamber in the last few years, that is, digital participation in the legislative process and Transparency 2.0, in order to observe their impasses and results obtained until now. In the first part the authors will study the e-Democracy portal and in the second part the authors will focus on open data, collaborative activities to use those data (hackathons) and the creation of the Hacker Lab, a permanent space dedicated to open parliament practices. The analysis considers the initiatives that the authors evaluated as part of the transformative and arena profiles of the Brazilian Parliament, according to Polsby's classification, with exclusive characteristics.

Introduction

The international programme Open Government Partnership (OGP) was launched in 2011 to provide a platform for helping national governments that were interested in becoming more open and responsive to the society they serve. The programme involves 65 countries in the world, including Brazil, which hosted the annual OGP discussion event in 2012. Many of the institutions of the Brazilian State are concerned with increasing availability of their data and making the participation of society in many instances of the political world possible.[1]

One of the institutions that is part of this movement in Brazil is the National Congress, by adapting this policy to the characteristic processes of the Legislative Power, a movement known as *Open Parliament*. The country is part of the Parliamentary Opening Declaration, signed in 2012 by 53 countries, which intends to encourage the opening of their parliaments through access to information about parliamentary activities, promoting transparency[2] and enabling a process of interaction between society and parliament.

In that sense, the Brazilian Chamber of Deputies has created several channels to enable the participation of society in the legislative process, understanding the participation as part of the process of representation. However, we have to emphasise that the channels were generally created on the initiative of the bureaucracy, even though in some cases, such as the ones we shall evaluate here, there has been some support of political agents.

The first step of this process was to increase transparency of its information, to later make the manifestation of the society through digital means feasible. The second step, that is, the biggest challenge that the institution faces right now, is to be able to respond to the manifestations that society has been sending, providing feedback to queries, suits, criticisms and other demands, also with the participation of parliamentarians. In some cases there has been an incorporation of citizens' suggestions into the legislative text.

It is in this context that the article presents an analysis of the implementation of an open parliament policy that is taking place in the Chamber of Deputies, in accordance with the guidelines of the OGP international programme, especially regarding the action plan of the Opening Parliament Work Group in particular, one of the subgroups of OGP. The definition of open government used will be the one by OGP itself: 'The transparency of government actions, the accessibility of government services and information, and the responsiveness of government to new ideas, demands and needs'.[3]

Frequently, an open government is considered equivalent to transparency, but this characteristic on its own is not enough. OGP states that citizens have to be able to obtain the necessary means so as to have something to say, to have the chance of influencing decision-making, and to fight for the accountability of such decisions. Meijer, Curtin, and Hillebrandt (2012) define an open government as a connection between voice and vision; that is, access to state information (*vision*), on the one hand, and the possibility to influence decision-making (*voice*), on the other. Therefore, open government – and, consequently, open parliament – implies transparency + participation (or engagement) + accountability.

In this article we adapt this 'open government' notion – much more directed to the Executive Branch – to parliament. Thus, the analysis will take place by means of a study of the 'Chamber of Deputies Hacker Lab', an office that includes Transparency 2.0 and social participation, through the e-Democracy portal, a channel for participation in the legislative process, considering its impasses and results obtained until now. The experiences will be analysed in the historic context of transparency and participation as an important level of the representation process, considering the theoretical collision that frequently happens between the streams that are included in this approach, with digital democracy experiments as an object for analysis.

In the theoretical key of this journal, the article intends to show, from the point of view of the bureaucracy (as its growth), mechanisms use according to the transformative profile in which, at first sight, the Brazilian Parliament would fit, according to a Polsby (1975) concept. According to this author (see Table 1), a transformative parliament would be one whose role in the phases of the legislative process would be relevant (through leaderships, commissions, plenary assemblies and remaining instances capable of affecting the wording of the legislative proposal, such as the participation channels) independently of the source of the legislative proposal. Therefore, this type of parliament would have a larger organisational structure. In this point we include the objects of analysis of this article, since transparency and political participation may affect the decision-making process in the various instances that this happens inside the parliament.

This profile would be opposite to the one defined by Polsby (1975) as an arena parliament, where the main focus of the legislative work is on the debate and the relationship between parties and pressure groups, with a low interference of parliament in the formulation and changes in the proposal itself, with law-making power; thus granting most of the power to the Executive Branch, who, in this case, would have a role as an institutor of the parliament. Therefore, it would have a smaller organisational structure.

Despite the role of the Executive Branch in Brazil being fairly relevant, we cannot affirm that the parliament does not exert a critical participation, since the parliamentary actions sometimes come to change, frequently, important wordings of proposals submitted by the Executive Branch itself, maybe exerting a more adequately reactive role, as more specifically defined by Cox and Morgenstern (2001). We shall see that, because contact with society is a desire that is more aligned with the bureaucracy, such an interface shows little political value, since it is not used by the parliamentarians during their political acts.

Table 1. Main characteristics of the arena and transformative parliaments, according to Polsby.

	Arena	Transformative
Focus of action	• Debating is more important than legislative work	• Relevant role in the several phases of the process (leaderships, commission, plenary assemblies, etc.)
Legislative result	• Low interference of the parliament in the formulation and modification of proposals	• High interference of the proposals in debate
Structure	• A more streamlined organisational structure	• Larger organisational structure

Note: Created by the authors.

We shall begin our approach with a theoretical reflection about the relationship between representation, social participation and transparency as a foundation for the idea of an open parliament. Soon, we shall analyse the e-Democracy portal for social participation in the legislative process, and the digital transparency experiences of the Chamber of Deputies, especially the open data initiatives, hackathons and the creation and workings of the Hacker Lab.

Open government and parliament in a context of representation, participation and transparency

The open government phenomena – transparency, participation and accountability – emerge at the height of the discussion about the dilemmas of representation and need (or lack of need) of more political participation. However old the tension between representative and participative democracies is, it took new proportions in the contemporaneity because of the greater social complexity in a context of ubiquity of the new technologies for information and communication (TICs).

The conflicts between the instances of political and social participation in the democratic regimes in several geographical and historical contexts are not new at all (Bobbio, 1987; Mouffe, 2000; Pateman, 1970), including the more recent Brazilian scenario (Avritzer, 2000; Nogueira, 2011; Rabat, 2010). The general issue is separated in exchanging representative democracy for participative democracy or merging participation with representation.

Deriving from the theoretical tradition based on the concept of popular sovereignty, participation is considered an instrument for the legitimisation and strengthening of the democratic institutions and the broadening of citizenship rights (Avelar, 2004). The issue of participation, however, has no consensus regarding its completion. Two currents form in their application: deliberative and participationist. In the deliberative current, participation should occur via rational debates, using instrumental reasoning, to come to a consensus regarding a certain subject, with the capacity to influence the actions of representatives. The emphasis is on political participation and democratisation of decision-making processes (Benhabib, 1996, p. 86). Therefore, it would not constitute a participation in the direct decision, but in the discussion process (and this process would be more valid than the result).

Publicity, reciprocity and accountability became essential aspects of the deliberative process (Gutmann & Thompson, 1996), which supports the concept of open government itself that we expose here. Thus, transparency becomes one of the main exponents of the deliberative democracy and it is strengthened in the current discussions about democracy, manifested in several current actions for access to information and open government.

118

Publicity that depends on transparency may encourage social and political participation, since, based on what is publicised about the representatives, the represented may react with an aim to interfere in the decision-making process. In the same way, when incited by the visibility of the demonstrations of civil society, representatives may define or reconfigure its political strategies for action in their electoral foundations or their tactics of action in the parliamentary activities (debates, elections, speeches, etc.)

Differently from the deliberative stream, the participationist one defends a direct participation in the decisions of the political environment (Barber, 2003; Pateman, 1970). More recently, some authors positioned themselves at an interface of this discussion (Avritzer, 2007; Dryzek & List, 2003; Lavalle, Houtzager, & Castello, 2006; Urbinati & Warren, 2008) with a view that participation does not exclude representation. This view is based on the conception that there is no crisis in the representative democracy, but in representation itself (Gomes, 2011), or, more specifically, problems in some aspects of representation that are inherent to it, therefore, named representation deficits (Fung, 2006).

According to this perspective, authors such as Nadia Urbinati (2005) defend an amplification of the concept of representation, including a participation in what she calls a negotiated representation, where the representatives should be able to be judged all the time, not just at the end of their terms. Thus, a continuous two-way bridge between parliament and society, increasing the transformative role of parliament when obtaining subsidies, and lasting legitimisation to modify decisions and/or projects.

It is in this context that we can position the so-called digital democracy. In general terms, we can say it is:

> Any sort of usage of devices (computers, cell phones, smartphones, palmtops, iPads …), applications (programs) and tools (forums, websites, social media …) of digital communication technologies to supplement, reinforce or correct aspects of the political and social practices of the State and its citizens, to benefit the democratic contents of the political community. (Gomes, 2011)

In the TICs environment, digital democracy formats the above-mentioned discussion and makes democratic mechanisms (Coleman & Blumler, 2009; Marques, 2008; Sampaio, 2010) such as the ones that will be focused upon in this article, transparency and participation, feasible. That happens because digital democracy is seen as a potential instrument for (Gomes, 2011, pp. 28–30): (1) strengthening the competitive capacity of citizenship (increasing proportion of citizen power, since competitive matches are permanent in politics); (2) consolidating and enforcing a Society of Rights, that is, an organised political community as a State of Rights (minorities); and (3) promoting an increase in the diversity of agents, agencies and agendas in the public sphere. In brief, offering broader possibilities to make the participative process feasible, a process seen here as a potential complement or improvement of the representative system.

Obviously we shall not disregard the problems that have already been pointed out about the so-called digital democracy or simply in the use of the internet for political education and information, e.g. calling it lesser political information, inequality in access to the media, lack of political culture, predominance of the action of means of mass communication as authorities in the virtual environment, excessive control and cyber threats, among others (Gomes, 2008, pp. 315–323). The objective of this article is solely to explore and critically analyse the open government instruments – tools, channels and processes – adapted to the institutional context of the Brazilian Chamber of Deputies.

From the aspect of transparency, some of the analysis of official parliamentary web portals has demonstrated an evolution in the information publication process in the managing and legislative terrains in the last few years, deliberately supporting popular participation, even though not by having direct participation in government or parliamentary decisions (Braga, 2007; Global Center for ICT in Parliaments, 2012). The publication of information about the expenses of the parliamentary term and the results of polls in the legislative sessions are examples, among many others, of information published in legislative portals.

The publication of open data[4] is a first step to Transparency 2.0 or digital transparency, which is the basis for the development of processes for understanding state action at a supplementary level and for deepening the tools offered by Transparency 1.0, that is, the sole publication of information in any format.

To leverage better the potential for the use of legislative data, public offices of many parts of the world have also supported civil initiatives to encourage collaborative development to obtain more efficiency in the final result of applications of transparency (Eyler-Werve & Carlson, 2012). These initiatives are carried in different formats, such as hackathons, hackdays, contests for ideas and applications and others.

Thus, the parliaments are able to contribute strongly to an increase in the transparency of the legislative process in several areas: (1) the publication of information in any format in their portals; (2) the availability of open data; (3) civil collaborative actions that encourage the use of these open data; and (4) the creation of permanent spaces and processes for a sustainable use and application of transparency actions, such as the creation of the Hack Lab at the Chamber of Deputies.

In the specific case of participation in the Brazilian Parliament, several channels for political manifestation and action of the citizen were created. In a country with continental dimensions (more than 8 million km^2) and with an equally large population (more than 200 million people) and a parliament that is located in the middle of the country and far from important decision-making centres in other states, instruments for participation become crucial to diminish the distance between parliamentarians and the population.[5]

Thus, the Brazilian Parliament has participation/deliberation instruments that range from comments in news of the communication channels of the Chamber of Deputies and participation in TV programmes at TV Câmara to the possibility to intervene directly in the legislative process through the e-Democracy portal, created in 2009, where forums and wikis are created to discuss legislative proposals that should be considered in the process of law-making.[6] Precisely because it has some impact in the legislative elaboration, our analysis will focus, based on participation, on the e-Democracy portal.

e-Democracy and participation in the legislature process

The e-Democracy channel of the Brazilian Chamber of Deputies, created in July 2009, is an example of the digital participation platform that is intended to encourage virtual discussion between citizens and parliamentarians during the legislative process. It has more than 35,000 registered members and 3000 discussion topics have been created,[7] alternating moments of great intensity of participation of citizens in the discussions with apathetic periods.[8]

Its main interaction vehicle is the portal, with many participation tools made available in the legislative virtual communities that are organised around specific legislative subjects. These instruments are considered multilateral channels, since they allow for a simultaneous interaction between citizens and deputies, with no restrictions regarding the number of accesses to the platform. They can be summarised in six tools with different conditions for dialogue and participation:

I. Wikilégis: tool for collaborative edition of legislative texts, through which citizens are able to comment on articles or proposals or suggest new wordings for legal devices;

II. Forum: asynchronous discussion environment where the subjects are more openly proposed (by any citizen) and discussed;

III. Legislative Virtual Community (CVL): a set of tools organised according to a discussion agenda. They are invoked by the parliamentarians themselves, who are committed to considering what was discussed when elaborating their reports (a movement from the inside out);

IV. Chat room: public hearings and parliamentary meetings might be broadcast online through these rooms, with the ability for a mediated interaction between deputies, experts and citizens.

V. Our Ideas: a tool that allows the participants to present their ideas or proposals for the solution of problems in just one sentence, as well as contributing to the ranking of the best idea. The final result is expressed through a number of reports, with the ranked list of the main ideas presented by those who take part.

VI. Freespace: where citizens can create, with no limitations or previous mediation, their own discussions (outside-in movement).

The statistical data from all of the six tools updated until 28 July 2015 allow us to have an idea of the quantitative use of the e-Democracy channel since its creation. Although the absolute access data are good (about 50 million accesses), we are not able to inform precisely how many people really have accessed the discussions at the e-Democracy portal. The chat room messages and forums are ranked higher because they work more freely and wikilégis, since it is the most recent tool, amounts to smaller numbers (Table 2).

Based on the data and the observation of the routine of the portal, we can see the small impact of discussions at Freespace, which functions more as an incubator for proposing subjects for discussion by the society and acts, therefore, as a way of mapping the topics considered relevant to the participants. There are no reports published in the portal that demonstrate follow-ups to the participations and responses from the parliamentarians, as there is with the CVLs. The CVLs encompass diverse subjects, such as the Brazilian Civil Rights Framework for the Internet, Youth Statute, climate change, space politics, etc.

A previous study (Faria, 2012) shows how these contributions were in fact used and leveraged in the elaboration of the final wordings, as noted in the acknowledgements of the Youth Statute. According to the rapporteur, Deputy Manuela D'ávila, in an interview given for the research, about 30 per cent of the text was based on the citizen suggestions that came from the e-Democracy portal. As an example, the rapporteur emphasises the section about the regulation of youth councils, a topic that was often tackled during the discussions, where citizens from places with very diverse social, political and economic contexts were able to give their opinion about the peculiarities of their region.

Table 2. e-Democracy numbers.

Accesses	49,455,668
Contributions to Wikilégis	2154
Virtual Legislative Communities	57
Messages in the chat rooms	19,503
Discussion topics created	4069
Forum participations	21,266
Ideas at 'Our Ideas'	518 ideas/217,014 votes

Note: Created by the authors.

In the discussion about the project for the Civil Rights Framework for the Internet, the rapporteur of the subject, Deputy Alessandro Molon, nominally pointed,[9] in each section of the substitute wording he presented, all the e-Democracy users who contributed to the construction of the device. More recently, the portal enabled the partition of citizens in the discussion of the political restoration inside the parliamentary work group created in 2013 to discuss the subject: more than 150,000 accesses, more than 3000 posts and more than 115,000 votes on a poll about the political restoration subjects (Cotrim, 2015).

However, participation gradually decreased throughout the life of the work group for political restoration, when only a few sparse mentions of the portal were made, without an actual repercussion of the manifestations of the people who used the website (Cotrim, 2015). Even so, the work group forum amassed 251,477 views, the largest number of visits to the e-Democracy portal, followed, with a big gap, by the virtual conference (a preparatory step of the 1st National Conference about Transparency and Social Control), with a total number of 6221 visits (Cotrim, 2015).

Generally speaking, even when there is no massive participation regarding more technical subjects, such as the regulation of the Unified Health System and the discussion about space policy, the few contributions are generally made by subject experts (and no common citizens, with no experience in the subject). They are very highly qualified, as certified by the legislative consultants of the subjects.[10] Some discussions had wide participation in some instances, with diverse objectives and a less direct impact in the final text, but resonated in the legislative process. That is exactly the case of the discussion about internet crimes. Because of the controversial nature of the theme, since it involves a great engagement of internet users, it fostered diverse contributions in the chats for the interactive public hearings, discussion forums and Wikilégis (Faria, 2014). This participation, despite its constraint, is only possible because of the data transparency and the access to the participation tool, which empowers citizens, and the ability to influence decisions, even though there is no direct participation in the decision-making process.

Since it is an interaction tool based in new technologies that evolve each day, e-Democracy has been facing important difficulties. The portal interface has been improved constantly; nonetheless, some improvements are still necessary regarding platform accessibility requirements, as well as a more user-friendly and intuitive navigation.

Several elements may affect the use of digital interaction channels such as e-Democracy by parliamentarians. They warrant a more refined research, but we can list some of the factors: age, experience with the use of digital tools, the human resources structure created to that end, and their policy-making ways, which is related to the old issue of term autonomy (the more permeable the term, the more parliamentarians might feel coerced to act according to the population, losing their autonomy to act in their best judgement[11]).

Between June 2009 and July 2015, less than 10 per cent of the 513 deputies participated in the portal in any way. One of the obstacles to increasing this process is the difficulty legislators have in handling the digital interaction tools and their incorporation in the parliamentary routine. The way parliamentarians have been reacting to this type of interaction with society is absolutely asymmetrical.

In addition to that, we found that parliamentarians face difficulties in blocking (or prioritising) time to post and debate with internet users at the e-Democracy portal. Some of them do it directly and without any help, that is, they access the portal, fill the initial registration and start participating, through a contribution in the discussion forums, and through participation in occasional chat rooms (one of the favourite tools of parliamentarians, because of their ease of use and immediate response to the participants).

Thus, we see that some parts of the material – reports, posts, etc. – of e-Democracy are able to support parliamentary work. This contributes both to an arena profile (see Table 1), because it broadens and strengthens debate – easing access to the pressure groups – and to a transformative profile, since it may support parliamentary reports in the most diverse phases of the legislative process. However, there is not a great engagement of deputies, that is, prioritisation by parliamentarians of this interface instrument. Considering e-Democracy as a supplement to the structural organisation of the Chamber and the fact that it turns this structure into a more complex one, e-Democracy would perfectly fit a transformative profile. Up to now, however, it still presents more potential (even though it is practically the only participation instrument that still is able to intervene somehow in the reports for law projects) than effective power to help transformation. In this way, both potentials end up very restricted.

Finally, it is still necessary to broaden the awareness of Brazilian society about the existence of the e-Democracy portal. During its six years of existence, it has had about 50 million accesses. Considering the current Brazilian population, which is in excess of 200 million people, there is plenty of space for gain. However, we have to stress its importance as a qualified participation instrument for society, with a potential for widening citizen participation. For that, it is obviously necessary still to make changes in Brazilian political culture, considered for a long time to be an apathetic culture with regards to politics, a perception that has changed in the last few years, especially after the globally recognised diverse demonstrations in 2013 and[12] the demonstrations regarding the impeachment of President Dilma Rousseff in 2015 and 2016.

In the following section, we shall start to draft the intensification of demands for legislative transparency, to be analysed in the scope of the work conducted by the Hacker Lab that is taking place simultaneously and with a crucial and direct relationship with political participation, analysed in this section regarding the e-Democracy portal.

Transparency 2.0 in the Brazilian Parliament

The Brazilian Chamber of Deputies has implemented, although in an incremental manner, a Transparency 2.0 policy through the availability of open legislative data and civil activities (hackathons, hackdays) to encourage its use. We can affirm that the great hallmark of the country in this area was the creation of the Access to Information Law in 2011. The law came into effect in May 2012 and created mechanisms that made it possible for any person, physically or legally, without any need to present a motivation, to obtain public information from offices and entities.

We shall now analyse the legislative transparency policy considering its impacts, challenges and advantages. We shall not limit our analysis to Transparency 1.0, simply based on publication of information and data in any format on the Chamber website and other official means (printed paper, government gazette, etc.), although other studies have also analysed the level of transparency of the Chamber in this point (Braga, 2007).

The focus of this part of the article is on Transparency 2.0, which involves the other three aspects previously exposed: open data, civil action and hacker space for collaboration and participation (LabHacker).

In December 2011, the Chamber of Deputies divulged a first package with legislative data in an open format, such as data from legislative proposals and plenarium agendas.[13] The next step was the creation of events and opportunities to stimulate civil society to use these data and to generate value based on them.

In the last week of October 2013, programmers, developers and experts in new technologies from all over the country met at the Chamber of Deputies in Brasilia to conduct the first Hackathon of the Brazilian Federal Legislative Branch, which would develop the Hacker Lab. Based on the data published by the Chamber, they created applications with the objective to improve the transparency of parliamentary work and to raise understanding of the legislative universe.[14]

The word itself, 'hackathon', is a symptom of the novelty character of the meeting. A neologism coming from cyber culture, the term is an abbreviation of the words hack + marathon, that is, a hacker marathon. During a couple of days, the attendees develop technological projects that can potentially contribute to the transparency of the Legislative Branch, crossing legislative data and showing them in an innovative, interactive and understandable way to any audience. Within this transparency concept, it is not enough that the parliaments make information and data about their operations available: they also have to encourage citizens (hackers, for example) to expose their own way of understanding the parliament, and, thus, facilitate the comprehension of other citizens.

This new proposition of contracts intends to change significantly the relationship between hacker movements and institutions. Previously seen as the *bad boys* of the web, when they invaded and stole corporations' and governmental websites, hackers today can be driving actors of the technological innovation in public and private institutions (Jordan & Taylor, 1998). The Chamber of Deputies, as well as other parliaments, has been gradually learning to leverage their potential for intelligence, versatility, creativity and boldness.

The first hackathon resulted in 27 transparency applications regarding parliamentary performance and usage of public resources to carry out the deputy terms. The second Chamber of Deputies hackathon, held from 24 to 28 November 2014, focused on another aspect, a specific public policy: gender issues (Melo, 2014).

During this marathon, hackers were encouraged to develop digital tools to help Brazilian society deal with subjects such as enforcement of gender public polices and political and representative participation by gender, a subject that has been a constant concern of a segment of political representatives and pro-gender activists. Brazil has high numbers of domestic violence suffered by women and only 7 per cent of women in the National Congress, despite the majority of the population being female.

Besides the subject and focus, another difference between the two hackathons was female participation. Among this group of 46, 23 of the attendees were women, an unusual number in activities that involved technology, especially the ones dominated by men. Women had a crucial role in the activity, as seen in the two winning applications, created by groups led by women. The projects developed during this hackathon encompassed applications with educational games about gender and reporting and mapping of violence, among others.

One of the most relevant aspects of the implementation of an open parliament policy is the permanent participation of society (at least a part of it) in the processes for social control of the institution. When following up on the interactions of the participants after the hackathon experiences, we could see that some of them came to interact among themselves, activating a collaboration network. For example, the hackers themselves have created a discussion group on Facebook[15] where they talk among themselves and with Chamber employees to improve the quality of open data, to promote the release of new data and to conduct other collective activities.

The hackathon experience catalysed a close contact between these youths and the universe of the democratic institutions. Both sides have won. The hackers learned, although in a superficial and limited manner, about the workings of a parliamentary democracy. The Chamber benefited from the creativity, experimentation, collaboration and agile culture of the programmers through the applications that were created.

During the hackathon living experiences, the participants had the opportunity to exchange ideas and talk to parliamentarians and employees of the Chamber of Deputies, which contributed to mutual learning and knowledge of other points of view of the political process, the bureaucracy of parliament and social control.

One case that illustrates the benefits of the approximation was a meeting between Deputy Paulo Pimenta and hackers who were developing a social control application about the parliamentary amendments to the federal budget. After getting to know the project during a conversation with one of its developers – activist Denis Moura – the deputy started showing possible paths for monitoring the amendments, using his parliamentary experience in presenting amendments to the budget and as the president of the Budget Commission of the National Congress in 2012. In the end, both came to some conclusions about how to proceed with the project in an efficient manner.[16]

In essence, the hackathon experiences have, in some way, helped reduce the tensions in the usual distrusting relationship between hackers and parliaments,[17] contributing to an arena aspect of the Legislative Branch (see Table 1) by promoting, widening and including society in the debate about the means of accessing information themselves and by making political participation subsequently easier, widening the discussion arena itself by facilitating access by a segment of the pressure groups.

This also contributes indirectly to empowering (but in this case it only empowers, it does not intervene, unlike e-Democracy) the transformative aspect of the Chamber. To be effective, this role will still depend on the use the parliamentarians make of the subsidies they come to receive. In this case, despite being part of a more supplementary structure, a more transformative profile, the Hacker Lab has, naturally, by its purpose for creation, a role in the debate.

We would also like to stress that one of the main aspects of the hackathons was the temporary establishment of the Chamber of Deputies as a coalescing centre for civil hackers, offering them a space for articulation. Despite the heterogeneity and lack of a strictly programmatic coordination of the movement, civil hackers had an opportunity to get to know each other and to organise actual proposals to present to the public power.

The most important result of these activities might have been the creation of a permanent open space for civil society inside the Chamber, the Hacker Lab, which creates conditions for continuity of the arena and transformative potentials we showed previously. During the 2013 hackathon, the president of the Chamber of Deputies, Deputy Henrique Eduardo Alves, interacted freely with the participants, answered questions and listened to commentaries. This meeting was broadcast online. One of the hackers requested the creation of a permanent space for collaboration between transparency activists, deputies and employees of the Chamber, which was observed promptly by the president. Later, the deputies approved the creation of the Hacker Laboratory in the Plenary Assembly.[18]

The relevant discussion to which we come now is: to what extent should a parliament go to engage citizens in collaborative actions that create a more open parliament, especially politics regarding transparency and social participation in the legislature process? Should society be introduced in the transformative role of the parliament? The raw materials for the creation of transformative transparency technologies are legislature data made available in open formats. Besides that, public institutions such as parliaments hold events to encourage and promote the use of data and generate new transparency values, such as applications that might, above all, increase the understanding of the population about the actual legislative work, or about how the parliamentarians use the resources at their disposal to conduct their term.

The great energy and effort exerted in a few days of work during a hackathon generated interesting results in terms of presented applications in the form of beta prototypes. On the other hand, issues to be resolved were also raised regarding these actions. The issues can be summed in two terms: *sustainability* and *reach*.

After the intense and exciting days of a collaborative event such as a hackathon, some of the applications that were presented are taken offline or simply will not work anymore. Problems mentioned by users are not solved anymore; there is no degree of service for the applications and they do not evolve, among other problems.

The reach of these results has also been very limited. Few parliamentarians know the applications and understand the new collaborative activities for transparency. There is some involvement by some parliamentarians, but not by parties or other legislative groups, such as commissions.

Ignorance of these technologies is also common among citizens and an even smaller part of society is effectively engaged in such actions. At the time of writing, collaborative transparency in the legislature is a very restricted niche activity.

Conclusions

The purpose of this article was to evaluate the main open parliament actions at the Brazilian Chamber of Deputies regarding the concepts of participation in the legislative process and transparency/collaborative government as ways to decrease democratic deficits by means of parliament, thus contributing to improvements to representative democracy.

In the case of the e-Democracy portal, where the citizen has an opportunity to intervene directly in legislative proposals, we observed that the portal has had about 50 million accesses since its creation, in 2009, an impressive number. This number can still increase when we consider the Brazilian population of more than 200 million inhabitants (more than 140 million voters, according to the Brazilian Superior Electoral Court). However, the potential for a quality contribution via political participation is real and represents a possibility for improvement of the legislative process itself.

The use of interactive tools is not a priority for most parliamentarians, both because of their lack of technological ability and because of their not regarding interfaces with society as important to their work. That is, the tool survives much more because of a bureaucratic determination than because of support and political use, even though those happen at some level. To that we might add the trepidation parliamentarians have about losing autonomy of their terms when they are under the scrutiny and influence of citizens. Thus, the transformative potential (of the Brazilian Parliament) does not happen with regards to leveraging the manifestations of society.

This participation process in the legislative process is complemented by the Transparency 2.0 actions conducted by the Hacker Lab. By leveraging the policy that determines the availability of legislative data in an open format by the Chamber of Deputies – even though the availability is gradual and mitigated – the civil actions for encouraging use and constructive processing of these data, such as hackathons and hackdays, are helping to improve the transparency processes of the legislative process. However, the collaborative development of transparency applications with the participation of citizens (civil hackers) is under evaluation, especially regarding its viability, sustainability and reach.

The social and political impact of these technological activities and subsequent applications is, therefore, still minimal. The lack of sustainability of groups or hacker-developer networks became evident. These actors participate erratically in civil actions, but after their completion they have serious difficulties in maintaining the developed applications, although some of them are working well and generating value in terms of the transparency of the Chamber.

Collaborative development, with the participation of citizens, parliamentarians and public officers, suggests a new model for the feasibility of transparency actions that, in the future, might bear more substantial and lasting fruit. We still have to know to what measure the consolidation of the work of the Hacker Lab will be able to effectively contribute to this process.

Nonetheless, as we observed, the process is more an institutional attitude of the bureaucracy in its beginnings, with a relative isolated participation of parliamentarians in e-Democracy, and successful results in interfering in the legislative process. This can be considered the most successful experience of the parliament–society interface (considering the parliament as its parliamentarians). In the case of the Hacker Lab the lack of connection with the political segment (parliamentarians) became evident, since the instrument is more of service to society and the administration of the House, although few parliamentarians are starting to participate in Hacker Lab activities.

It becomes clear, therefore, as pointed out in both cases, that the tools have a potential for broadening the arena profile (because of their potential for widening and improving the debate and increasing the access of pressure groups) in the Brazilian Parliament, as well as transformative or reactive elements (because they increase and legitimise the possibility of formulating and changing the proposed policies with the population, since it is able to support the legislative and decision-making processes of the House). Nevertheless, this practically does not happen or happens in a rudimentary (though successful) manner, in the case of e-Democracy.

The current situation reveals a complex and sophisticated structure that still does not identify clearly the related parties, and, therefore, constrains its own potential. It also does not guarantee more legitimacy to parliamentary work, which would support it is as transformative parliament. More research is warranted in regards to knowing whether this is a process that tends to mature and become more consolidated, fulfilling the dialogue of society and parliament as equally strong actors, or whether it will be gradually unmade by the parliamentary culture that is still not fully convinced of the potential of the tools for participation and transparency. This actual demand increases every day for Brazilian society, after the 2013 demonstrations and amidst the massive political-institutional crisis that has been taking place in the country ever since the presidential elections of 2014.

Notes

1. For more information, see http://www.opengovpartnership.org/.
2. For more information, see www.openingparliament.org.
3. May be accessed at http://www.opengovguide.com/glossary/. Last accessed 3 April 2015.
4. The definition of open data encompasses basically eight principles defined by a group of experts and government transparency activists. A certain set of data published online should be considered 'open' if it is: thorough, primary, current, accessible, machine-processed, non-discriminatory, non-proprietary and unlicensed. For more information, visit https://opengovdata.org/.
5. Even more so if we consider the proportional electoral system, which, on its own, is enough to hamper accountability processes, despite raising representativeness.
6. For more information about these channels, see the article by Teixeira, Bernardes, and Rodrigues in this issue.
7. Data collected in July 2015.

8. Available at the icon 'Participe' on the home page of the Chamber (www. camara.leg.br), or directly (www.edemocracia.leg.br). You just have to register quickly to access the tools offered.
9. Here we present the board with the respective suggestions of citizens incorporated to the final text presented by Deputy Alessandro Molon. This board is part of the opinion presented by Deputy Molon, (http://goo.gl/GxiZ67). Last accessed 18 April 2016.
10. The Legislative Consultancy of the Chamber consists of experts in 21 knowledge areas in public policy such as health, education, labour, etc. These are professionals who underwent national public service exams, and, after three years on the job, acquired tenure. They are not, therefore, attached to any political parties.
11. Pitkin defines this debate very well in *The Concept of Representation* (1967).
12. The demonstrations of 2013 are known for millions of Brazilian having taken to the streets, initially because of the rise in bus fares, but later having evolved to important subjects in national politics, such as corruption. They were not linked to parties and were organised mainly through social media.
13. Available at http://www2.camara.leg.br/transparencia/dados-abertos. Last accessed 4 March 2015.
14. For more details of the regulation and applications developed in the hackathons in 2013 and 2014, see http://www2.camara.leg.br/responsabilidade-social/ edulegislativa/educacao-legislativa-1/educacao-para-a-democracia-1/ hackathon/2014/hackaton2014. About the applications, see http://labhackercd. net/hackathon.html#hackathons. Last accessed 4 March 2015.
15. The Facebook group Hackathon – Maratona Hacker – Câmara dos Deputados is an example of this and can be accessed at https://www.facebook.com/groups/ 451738954947012/. Last accessed 28 July 2015.
16. The conversation between the deputy and the Hackathon participant can be watched in this video: https://www.youtube.com/watch?v=XEcSCkttI3w. Last accessed 28 July 2015.
17. Government transparency activists, and civil hackers, a subgroup of them, tend to present a critical rather than collaborative posture regarding the state because of the common resistance in politicians and bureaucrats to actualise transparency actions.
18. For more information, see www.labhackercd.net. Last accessed 4 March 2015.

Disclosure statement

No potential conflict of interest was reported by the authors.

References

Avelar, L. (2004). Participação política [Political participation]. In: L. Avelar & A. O. Cintra (Orgs.), *Sistema político: uma introdução* [Political systems: An introduction] (pp. 23–35). São Paulo: UNESP.

Avritzer, L. (2000). Teoria democrática e deliberação pública [Democratic theory and public deliberation]. *Lua Nova, 49*, 25–46. doi:10.1590/S0102-64452000000200003. Retrieved from http://www.scielo.br/scielo.php?pid=S0102-64452000000200003&script= sci_abstract&tlng=pt

Avritzer, L. (2007). Sociedade Civil, Instituições Participativas e Representação: da Autorização à Legitimidade da ação [Civil Society, Participative Institutions and Representation: From authorization to Legitimacy of action]. *Dados*, Rio de Janeiro. *50*(3), 443–464.

Barber, B. (2003). *Strong democracy – participatory politics for a new age.* Berkeley: University of California Press.

Benhabib, S. (1996). Toward a deliberative model of democratic legitimacy. In S. Benhabib (Ed.), *Democracy and difference: Contesting the boundaries of the political* (pp. 67–94). Princeton: Princeton University Press.

Bobbio, N. (1987). *Estado, governo, sociedade: para uma teoria geral da política* [State, government, society: For a general theory of politics]. Rio de Janeiro: Paz e Terra.

Braga, S. (2007). *O Papel das TICs na Institucionalização das Democracias: um estudo sobre a informatização dos órgãos legislativos na América do Sul com destaque para o Brasil* [The Role of ICTs in Institutionalization of Democracies: A study on the computerization of the legislative bodies in South America with emphasis on Brazil]. Brasília: Edições Câmara.

Coleman, S., & Blumler, J. G. (2009). *The internet and democratic citizenship: Theory, practice and policy.* Cambridge: Cambridge University Press.

Cotrim, A. (2015). *Repercussões da participação popular na tramitação da reforma política na Câmara dos Deputados* [Repercussions of popular participation in the conduct of political reform in the Brazilian Chamber of Deputies] (Master's thesis) (not published)presented in August, 2015, as part of a Professional Master's in Legislature of the Chamber of Deputies Brasília, Brazil. Retrieved from http://bd.camara.leg.br/bd/handle/bdcamara/27199

Cox, G. W., & Morgenstern, S. (2001). Latin America's reactive assemblies and proactive presidents. *Comparative Politics, 33*(2), 171–189. Retrieved from http://isites. harvard.edu/fs/docs/icb.topic925740.files/Week%208/Cox_Latin.pdf

Dryzek, J., & List, C. (2003, December). Social choice theory and deliberative democracy: A reconciliation. *Political Science, 33*, 1–28.

Eyler-Werve, K., & Carlson, V. (2012). *The civic apps competition handbook.* Sebastopol, CA: O'Reilly Media.

Faria, C. F. S. (2012). *O Parlamento aberto na Era da Internet: pode o povo colaborar com o Legislativo na elaboração das leis?* [The open parliament in the age of the internet: Can the people now collaborate with legislatures in lawmaking?]. Brasília: Edições Câmara.

Faria, C. F. S. (2014). Participação popular na elaboração de leis: análise do Projeto e-Democracia da Câmara dos Deputados [Popular participation in the drafting of laws: Analysis of the project and Democracy House of Representatives]. In E. S. M. Cunha & H. D. Theodoro (Eds.), *Desenho Institucional, Democracia e Participação: Conexões Teóricas e Possibilidades Analíticas* [Institutional design, Democracy and Participation: Theoretical Connections and Analytical Possibilities] (pp. 155–176). Belo Horizonte: D'Plácido.

Fung, A. (2006). Democratizing the policy process. In R. E. Goodin, M. Moran, & M. Rein (Eds.), *The Oxford handbook of public policy* (pp. 667–683). Oxford: Oxford University Press.

Global Center for ICT in Parliaments. (2012). World e-Parliament Report 2012. Retrieved from http://www.ictparliament.org/WePReport2012.html

Gomes, W. (2011). Participação política online: questões e hipóteses de trabalho [Online political participation: Questions and working hyphoteses]. In R. Maia, W. Gomes, & F. Marques (Orgs.), *Internet e Participação Política no Brasil* [Internet and Political Participation in Brasil]. Porto Alegre, Brazil: Editora Sulina.

Gomes, W. (2008). Internet e participação política [Internet and political participation]. In W. Gomes & R. Maia (Eds.), *Comunicação e Democracia* [Communication and democracy] (pp. 292–326). São Paulo: Paulus.

Gutmann, A., & Thompson, D. F. (1996). *Democracy and disagreement.* Cambridge, MA: Belknap Press of Harvard University Press.

Jordan, T., & Taylor, P. (1998, November). A sociology of hackers. *Sociological Review, 46*(4), 757–780.

Lavalle, A. G., Houtzager, P. P., & Castello, G. (2006). Democracia, pluralização da representação e sociedade civil [Democracy, pluralization of representation and civil society]. *Lua Nova: Revista de Cultura e Política, 67*, 49–103.

Marques, F. P. J. A. (2008). *Participação Política e Internet: Meios e Oportunidades Digitais de Participação Civil na Democracia Contemporânea, com um Estudo do Caso do Estado Brasileiro* [Political Participation and Internet: Media and Digital Opportunities of Civil Participation in Contemporary Democracy, with a Brazilian State Case Study]. Salvador, BA: Faculdade de Comunicação, Universidade Federal da Bahia. Retrieved from http://www.repositorio.ufc. br:8080/ri/bitstream/123456789/671/1/2008_tese_%20fpjamarques.pdf

Meijer, A. J., Curtin, D., & Hillebrandt, M. (2012). Open government: Connecting vision and voice. *International Review of Administrative Sciences, 78*(1), 10–29.

Melo, M. R. M. (2014, November 24). Hackathon de Gênero e Cidadania [Gender and citizenship hackathon]. *Congresso em Foco.* Retrieved from http:// congressoemfoco.uol.com.br/opiniao/forum/hackathon-de-genero-cidadania-da-camara/

Mouffe, C. (2000). *The democratic paradox.* London: Verso.

Nogueira, M. A. (2011). *Um estado para a sociedade civil* [An state for civil society]. São Paulo, Brazil: Cortez.

Pateman, C. (1970). *Participation and democratic theory.* Cambridge: Cambridge University Press.

Polsby, N. W. (1975). Legislatures. In F. I. Greenstein & N. Polsby (Orgs.), *Handbook of political science.* USA: Addison-Wesley. Retrieved from http://works.bepress. com/nelson_polsby/18/

Rabat, M. N. (2010). *Representação, participação política e controle social: instituições, atores e história* [Representation, political participation and social control: Institutions, actors and history]. Biblioteca Digital da Câmara dos Deputados. Retrieved from http://www2.camara.leg.br/documentos-e-pesquisa/publicacoes/estnottec/areas-da-conle/tema3/2009_9987.pdf

Sampaio, R. (2010). Participação Política e os Potenciais Democráticos da Internet [Political participation and Internet Democratic Potencials]. *Revista Debates, 4* (1), 29–53.

Urbinati, N. (2005, September). *O que torna a representação democrática* [What makes representation democratic]. Text presented at the American Political Science Association (Apsa) Annual Meeting, Washington (EUA). Translated by Mauro Soares. Retrieved from http://www.scielo.br/pdf/ln/n67/a07n67.pdf

Urbinati, N., & Warren, M. (2008, September). The concept of representation in contemporary democratic theory. *Annual Review of Political Science, 11,* 387–412.

Conclusion

Cristiane Brum Bernardes, Cristina Leston-Bandeira and Ricardo de João Braga

ABSTRACT
This special issue has discussed the wider representative role of the Brazilian Parliament's lower chamber, the Chamber of Deputies, through an analysis that has integrated the way it processes policy with how it communicates with citizens. Adopting as an overarching framework, Polsby's typology on Arena vs. Transformative legislatures, the articles have discussed the institutionalisation process of the Chamber of Deputies, its role within the political process and its relationship with other political institutions, the policy-making process, new communication and information technologies used by the Chamber of Deputies and its capacity to promote interaction between citizens and parliament. The findings show that policy-making and communication capacities have grown in so far as democracy lasts. Another important finding relates to the crucial role played by the administrative body of the Chamber of Deputies, which acts itself as the key interactive link between citizens and parliament, to the point that it takes over the representatives' role.

Parliament's role

This issue of *The Journal of Legislative Studies* has analysed the wider representative role of the Brazilian Chamber of Deputies, in contemporary Brazil. It has sought to present its history and discuss the operation of this legislative house, clarifying its role as a decision-maker on public policy and as a promoter of the interaction between the political system and citizens.

The issues

The two key issues that structure the collection relate to the role of the Chamber of Deputies in the development of public polices and in the promotion of interaction between the political system and citizens. We questioned both the effective performance of said roles and the conditions in which these activities are performed, emphasising the internal structure of the Chamber of Deputies and its capacity to promote these actions.

Both issues are, in fact, consequences of the basic problem related to democracy and representation. Brazil, a country with a political history punctuated by several institutional ruptures and periodical suppressions of representative democracy, has built a Chamber of Deputies that is a consequence of this process (since it faces the fragility of the partisan system and of the democratic values and practices). However, the institution seeks also to become an influence in the political system as a whole, especially in political communication actions.

The theoretical basis of Polsby (1975) makes sense in this case, since it allows for both an articulation of the role of a policy-maker (in the transformative legislative role) and a role of political communication with the citizens (in the arena legislative role). It is also important to emphasise that Polsby's perspective enlightens the internal organisation of the Legislative Branch, which, in the case of Brazil, is crucial due to the sheer size of these structures and the role they perform in the dynamics of the activities of the Chamber of Deputies.[1]

We also would like to highlight the diversity of theoretical and empirical perspectives about the Legislature presented in this issue, a result of the different backgrounds of the authors, the different disciplines used for reflection (history, political science, sociology, business administration, communication, among others), and also of different methodologies adopted to analyse the legislative phenomenon. If the historical dimension of the political role of the Brazilian Congress might lead us to a pessimistic vision of the power of the parliamentary institution over the political process, as presented by Pinto and Sathler et al., on the other hand, the empirical analysis of the activities linked to educational policies and health funding by Gomes and Martins or of the resistance of the environmentalist core, as demonstrated by Schneider and Marques, as well as a greater involvement with the communication role, transforms the contemporary relationship between the Executive and Legislative Branches of power in Brazil into a picture in several shades of grey.

Answers and unfolding

The historical past and the contemporary configuration of the Chamber of Deputies point to a process of growing importance of the Legislative Branch, a characteristic that is consistent with the evolution of Brazilian democracy, which, currently, is in its longest period of existence. Democratic life strengthens the Legislative Branch, which has been growing in influence in the making of policies and in a greater interaction with society.

Active, reactive, collaborative and innovative, in the terms put forth by Ferri and Rodrigues, the Brazilian Parliament has undergone an evolution process throughout the years, due to the growing complexity of the internal structure and of the roles performed within the political system. This complexity can be expressed in the difficulty of positioning it in the spectrum created by Polsby between the transformative and arena types of legislature. In fact, from the theoretical and empirical perspectives we adopted, the Brazilian Congress can be characterised more as a transformative one or more typically a political arena, in different moments of its history.

The articles of this special issue of *The Journal of Legislative Studies* reach two conclusions. The first one is that the organisational structure of the Chamber of Deputies is substantial, in terms of financial and human resources, and is oriented towards performing some roles almost in place of what is expected of the actions of parliamentarians. This introduces important questions regarding legitimacy of political decision-making, as it is the parliamentarian who is elected, rather than the official; these questions are particularly important in a political system that has undergone a number of transitions between autocratic and democratic systems. The institutional involvement of the Chamber in activities for communication with society is significant, both in a journalistic aspect and in the interaction within the legislative process. This ample structure is, moreover, supportive to the individual careers of the parliamentarians. This happens both because of the exposure the deputies receive within the actions of the Chamber of Deputies and the direct support to their individual careers, with support staff, office space and resources for communication activities with voters (transportation, mail, telephone, websites, etc. all of this being covered by the state).

The second conclusion, about the process of creation of public policies and also about the governance abilities of the Chamber of Deputies, is that it is in a medium place of influence, in which the great player is the Executive Branch. This medium placement, however, should still be considered under a historical perspective, according to what Pinto and Sathler et al. show. During the Republic, for two extensive periods the Legislative Branch was suppressed from the public arena as a relevant actor. During the Vargas dictatorship (1937–45), the National Congress simply did not operate. During the Military Dictatorship (1964–85), the Congress was kept in operation; however, it was destitute of many its prerogatives (Packenham, [1970] 1990). The current democratic period, which completed 30 years in 2015 (if we mark its beginning with the election of the first civilian after the military regime in 1985), is characterised as a relatively new process of interaction between the Legislative and Executive Branches, and it seems to stimulate and strengthen the representative institution.

We can discern that the Chamber of Deputies has been moving towards new means of interaction. On one hand, its organisational capacities have grown with time, as stated by Sathler, Braga and Miranda. On the other hand, the manner of the relationship between the Legislative and Executive Branches, especially the control of members, has grown in importance in the public debate.

We can also see greater concerns about the Legislative Branch emerging from society, since some public debates, which are impossible to solve under the coordination of the Executive Branch, have lent some vigour to the Legislative Branch and given it more importance in the public debate. For example, the issues of education, health and environment, treated in this compilation, are themes of growing importance among voters and public opinion – and even within the Executive Branch, the key agenda-setter, they are not consensual in many cases, a characteristic that adds value to the legislative debate.

When considering the structure of the Brazilian legislature from an internal and historical perspective, as well as its roles in the political system and its *raisons d'être*, this special issue allows the reader to raise a hypothesis that is mentioned in the texts. If the criticism of the Legislative made by society appears as a practically omnipresent characteristic of democracies, the Brazilian case demonstrates that this criticism has generated structural/organisational responses to political/behavioural issues. In other words, the Legislative augments its size and its bureaucratic structure to increase or replace roles that could or should be performed by the parliamentarians themselves in the traditional representation contexts (partisan and electoral activities). Examples presented in this issue are the communication and approximation activities between parliamentarians and citizens, to which the House expends a considerable managerial and financial effort.

In this sense, autonomy of the Legislature for policy-making and promotion of the interaction between the political system and citizens are not exclusive goals in complex and diverse contemporary societies such as Brazil. The contact with society and the engagement of the citizens with parliament may be irreversible, not only due to the efforts exerted by the legislative bureaucracy to open channels for interaction, as shown by Barros et al. and Ferri and Rodrigues, but much more due to the social demand itself for transparency and accountability. Thus, the dimensions presented by Polsby, despite their relevance, must exist combined.

How the political actors – representatives and citizens – will deal with these new configurations and institutional possibilities in Brazil is a subject for more research and reflection on the part of those interested in the improvement of democratic regimes and legislatures.

Note

1. The data and reality discussed in this collection are prior to 2016 and the internal unfolding of the political crisis experienced by the country throughout the last 12 months. Thus, we were not concerned with analysing the changes that the structure went through during this boisterous period, or the consequences these changes may exert on the legislative process as a whole. An

exception to this was the paper authored by Pinto, which approached some of these transformations, even though it did so through a more general point of view for the Brazilian political system as a whole.

Disclosure statement

No potential conflict of interest was reported by the authors.

References

Packenham, R. A. (1990). Legislatures and political development. In P. Norton (Ed.), *Legislatures* (pp. 81–95). Oxford: Oxford University Press.
Polsby, N. W. (1975). Legislatures. In F. I. Greenstein & N. W. Polsby (Ed.), *Governmental institutions and processes* (pp. 257–317). Handbook of Political Science, Volume 5. Reading, MA: Addison-Wesley Publishing Company.

Index

For Product Safety Concerns and Information please contact our EU
representative GPSR@taylorandfrancis.com
Taylor & Francis Verlag GmbH, Kaufingerstraße 24, 80331 München, Germany

www.ingramcontent.com/pod-product-compliance
Ingram Content Group UK Ltd.
Pitfield, Milton Keynes, MK11 3LW, UK
UKHW021437080625
459435UK00011B/292